ON
AFRICAN
SOCIALISM

ON
AFRICAN
SOCIALISM

Léopold Sédar Senghor

Translated and with an Introduction by
MERCER COOK

FREDERICK A. PRAEGER, *Publisher*
New York • London

FREDERICK A. PRAEGER, PUBLISHER
64 UNIVERSITY PLACE, NEW YORK 3, N.Y., U.S.A.
77-79 CHARLOTTE STREET, LONDON W. 1, ENGLAND

The first two essays in this volume were first published in French in 1961 under the title *Nation et Voie Africaine du Socialisme,* and in 1962, in an English translation, under the title *Nationhood and the African Road to Socialism,* by Présence Africaine.

Published in the United States of America in 1964
by Frederick A. Praeger, Inc., *Publisher*

Library of Congress Catalog Card Number: 64-16419

Printed in the United States of America

Introduction

On November 3, 1961, President Kennedy welcomed President Senghor to the White House with these words: "A famous American once said many years ago that he did not care who wrote his nation's laws so long as he could write this nation's songs. Mr. President, you help write your nation's songs and poems, and you also help write your nation's laws. You have been an architect of your country's independence. You have been the poet in the sense of the aspirations of the people of Africa."

The unusual gifts of Senegal's poet-statesman make him unique among world leaders. In this connection, a recent biographer, Armand Guibert, without passing judgment on Senghor's political talents, wonders whether Plato underestimated poets in his ideal *Republic*. Though few bards have achieved lasting success in the political arena, Guibert directs our attention to this quotation from Henri Fauconnier:

> If this were not a topsy-turvy world, it would be governed by poets, for they are the most lucid of men. Beneath the appearances and conventions that blind us, they alone see reality in all its richness, its depth, its instability. Their glance is clear and ever new. They see and they foresee. All human discoveries, religions, and revolutions are their handiwork, albeit occult.*

* Armand Guibert, *Léopold Sédar Senghor* (Paris: Seghers, 1961), p. 45.

v

But the architect of Senegalese independence is more than a poet-statesman. He is also a teacher. The imprint of his first profession is evident throughout these pages, as it has been throughout his career. In a letter of May 18, 1963, he writes, to justify his use and repetition of certain basic quotations: "I am still a professor and I like to drive in nails [i.e., drive home my points]."

What, one may ask, is Senghor trying to teach in these three essays on nationhood, African socialism, and Senegalese socialism? Briefly, he wants to show how Senegal can become a modern, democratic nation-state. The answer is not a simple one, for the problems are numerous and complex. The integration of *Négritude*—defined in the third essay as "the common denominator of all Negro Africans"*—and socialism requires special directives that only the theoretician of *Négritude* and African socialism can furnish. On the local level, a sense of nationhood must be developed among the various ethnic and social groups that comprise the population. Economic, political, and cultural reforms must provide new opportunities and new hope for the masses, 80 per cent of whom are peasants. On the international scene, Senegal must continue to seek closer ties with its African neighbors, despite the temporary setback caused by the rupture of the Mali Federation in August, 1960.† Cooperation with the

---

* For a more detailed definition, see Senghor's *Pierre Teilhard de Chardin et la politique africaine* (Paris: Editions du Seuil, 1962), p. 20:

Négritude is simply the totality of civilizing values of the Negro world. It is not racism, but culture; it is a situation understood and overcome in order to integrate and harmonize with the cosmos. As a symbiosis of determining factors—geographical and ethical—*Négritude* becomes rooted in these factors by taking on an original color, but historically it does so to transcend them, just as life transcends the matter from which it springs.

† On January 17, 1959, the Sudanese Republic (formerly the French Sudan) had joined with Senegal to form the Mali Federation. Modibo Keita, of the Sudanese Republic, was its Prime Minister, while Senghor served as President of the National Assembly and head of the Party of African Federation. The federal experiment was abandoned on August 20, 1960: Modibo Keita returned to Bamako, where he became head of the Mali Republic (the new name taken by the Sudanese Republic); Senghor was elected President of Senegal. Throughout this book, "Sudan" refers to what is now the present state of Mali, formerly the French Sudan, and *not* to the former Anglo-Egyptian Sudan, now the Republic of Sudan.

former colonizer must be maintained on an egalitarian basis to the advantage of both countries. Nevertheless, Senegal must pursue a policy of nonalignment to avoid involvement in the Cold War.

Those who consider his attitude too moderate or too pro-French forget that Senghor publicly advocated independence as early as 1946. Interviewed in *Gavroche* on August 8 of that year, he assured "the whites of our unshakable determination to win our independence. . . . It would be both foolish and dangerous for them to try to hold back the clock. We are ready, if need be as a last resort, to conquer freedom by all means, not excluding violence. I do not believe that France, which has just eliminated Hitlerian racism, can blame us for this decision." And yet Senghor realizes that nationhood is only the first step on the road to a global civilization. Repeatedly, he refers to the "Civilization of the Universal" to which all peoples will contribute,* and which will be unattainable unless narrow nationalism is transcended. He has long been an apostle of unity, an opponent of the balkanization that has helped to retard his continent economically and politically. With the failure of his first attempt at a regional federation, he made a fresh start when he led Senegal into a looser grouping with twelve nations in the Union of African States and Madagascar, then with twenty nations in the Monrovia Group, and subsequently, in May, 1963, into the 32-nation Organization of African Unity created at Addis Ababa. Meanwhile, through its relations with France, the Common Market, the United Nations, and men of good will everywhere, Senegal hopes to participate in the building of a peaceful, more prosperous world.

Senghor's approach is eclectic. Retaining such traditional African values as religion and the community spirit,† Senegal, he

* Significantly, the title of one of Senghor's earliest essays is "What the Black Man Brings," in the symposium *L'Homme de couleur* (Paris: Plon, 1939); see p. 314: "The Negro will have contributed, with other peoples, to reforging the unity of man and the world: linking the flesh to the spirit, man to fellow man, the pebble to God."

† According to a French Africanist, "the essential social indication of their *Négritude*, contrasting with our individualism of Greek origin, is their community-mindedness." *Hommage à Jacques Richard-Molard* (Paris: Présence Africaine, 1953), p. 63.

believes, must develop its "open," "democratic," "humanistic" socialism, selecting and applying the most useful contributions available. From French Utopian socialists it will borrow trade unionism and the cooperative. From Marxism-Leninism it will accept dialectics but reject atheistic materialism. It will have a planned economy with a public, a mixed, and a private sector. Nationalization as well as *laissez-faire* will be avoided. Techniques and technicians from France and other developed countries will be welcome, and an intensive program to train African cadres will be instituted. The basic prerequisite is that these various devices be applicable to twentieth-century Negro-African realities; without meeting this criterion, Senghor believes, no prefabricated foreign model designed for other times and other people can suffice. Africa in general and Senegal in particular must find their own road to socialism, just as the Scandinavians, Israelis, and Yugoslavs have done:

> We have not allowed ourselves to be seduced by Russian, Chinese, or Scandinavian models. After an objective examination, we have learned lessons from the successes and failures of the different "socialist experiments." Above all, we have observed that formulas like "priority for heavy industry" or "agrarian reform" have no magic power within themselves; applied dogmatically, they have produced partial failures.

By the same token, Senghor rejects other Communist slogans, such as "the dictatorship of the proletariat." At one point he accuses those who use it of simply "gargling a formula." At another point he declares, "In the Communist countries, the 'dictatorship of the proletariat,' contrary to the teachings of Marx, has made the state an omnipotent, soulless monster, stifling the natural freedoms of the human being and drying up the sources of art, without which life is not worth living." Obviously, this formula and the theory of the class struggle would not apply to a proletarian country such as Senegal, where, Senghor insists, "There are no classes at war, but social groups struggling for influence." Once again, Black Africa must determine its policies and priorities in the light of its own realities.

This critical, objective spirit, so characteristic of the conscientious teacher, impels Senghor to make a thorough study of Marxism-Leninism, which he discusses at length in the first and third essays. His painstaking analysis of the major works of Marx, Engels, and Lenin enables him to reveal the strengths and weaknesses of scientific socialism and to explain why—for theoretical and practical reasons—Communism is not the answer to Africa's problems. "We can no longer accept Marx's vision of the future," he declares, thereby anticipating a statement that a distinguished American, Ambassador Chester Bowles, made on April 29, 1963: "As a matter of simple fact, the world is refusing to act as Communist ideology said it would or should—and the Communists can't cope with it."

As one corrective to the dogmatic one-sidedness of Communist materialism, Senghor proposes the well-rounded philosophical and scientific theories of Father Pierre Teilhard de Chardin. He quotes at length from the Jesuit's *Phenomenon of Man,* which Sir Julian Huxley introduced to English and American readers as "a very remarkable book by a very remarkable human being." Sir Julian predicted that Teilhard's "influence on the world's thinking is bound to be important. Through his combination of wide scientific knowledge with deep religious feeling and a rigorous sense of values, he has forced theologians to view their ideas in the new perspective of evolution, and scientists to see the spiritual implications of their knowledge." Teilhard pictures humanity as evolving toward "ultra-reflection," the planetary civilization, convergence with the Omega point (God). In this way, man will realize his full potential and progress from well-being to maximum-being. For the Senegalese who, Senghor reminds us, have not yet attained well-being and who are still suffering from poverty, disease, and ignorance, there are more immediate objectives. Nevertheless, Teilhard's theory, based on the latest scientific discoveries, leaves room for God and does not consider religion "the opium of the masses." Essentially religious, like the overwhelming majority of Africans, the Senegalese learn in these lectures that their socialism will not be incompatible with the teachings of Jesus and Mohammed. To emphasize this point, Senghor quotes the Bible, the Koran, and a number of Islamic and Christian commentators.

In fact, one of the most impressive aspects of this book is the amazing range of Senghor's erudition. From Heraclitus to Hegel, from Marx to Mauriac, from Engels to Einstein, from Lincoln to Lenin, from François Perroux to Gaston Berger, from Teilhard to Gaëtan Picon, he cites passages that one would hardly expect to hear analyzed at an African political rally. Refusing to "Africanize at a discount," he shuns neither the difficult nor the unpopular.* Always the teacher, he has the patience to explain, the intellectual honesty not to oversimplify, and faith that the lesson will be understood.

Though intended primarily for his compatriots, the lesson has relevance for the rest of the world as well. It serves notice of Senegal's determination to follow its own course to economic progress and human dignity, with friendship for all and slavish imitation of none. "What good is our independence," Senghor asks, "if it is only to imitate European totalitarianism, to replace external colonialism with domestic colonialism?" Eagerness to cooperate with foreign nations should by no means be interpreted as willingness to accept dictation from abroad. The days of tele-guided institutions and decisions for most of Africa are no more. Similarly, Senghor's observations on race relations, African culture, the Bandung Conference, etc., should enlighten anyone who may cherish the illusion that the *status quo ante* can be restored.

The author has relatively little to say about the United States. He knows, of course, that the major threat to a world of free choice does not come from the West. Hungary, Tibet, the Berlin Wall, and the Chinese invasion of India are glaring examples of this truth. Though unmentioned in these essays, they are too ominous to have escaped the notice of the perceptive African leader. In the final analysis, the real danger for Africa and other underdeveloped areas comes from the gullibility and desperation

---

* Note, for example, in the second essay, his admission that colonialism produced benefits as well as evils:

Let us stop denouncing colonialism and Europe and attributing all our ills to them. Besides not being entirely fair, this is a negative approach, revealing our inferiority complex, the very complex the colonizer inoculated in us. . . . It is too easy an alibi for our own laziness, for our selfishness as intellectuals, for our failures. It would be more positive for us and our people to analyze the colonial fact objectively, while psychoanalyzing our resentment.

of those who may be deluded into believing that Communism is universally valid.* Accordingly, Senghor devotes much of his attention here to the basic educational task of revealing the true nature of Communism and of offering his constituents a surer, more human road to progress. To repeat, this road will be neither Russian nor American, but *African:*

> The paradox in the building of socialism in Communist countries, or at least in the Soviet Union, is that it increasingly resembles capitalistic growth in the United States, the American way of life, with high salaries, refrigerators, washing machines, and television sets, but with less art and less freedom of thought. Nevertheless, we shall not be won over to a regime of liberal capitalism and free enterprise. We cannot close our eyes to segregation, although the Federal Government combats it, nor can we accept material success as a way of life. We stand for a middle course, for a *democratic socialism,* which goes so far as to integrate spiritual values, a socialism which ties in with the old ethical current of the French socialists.

The idea of Senegalese or African socialism is bitter gall to the Communists, who are taught to take their Marxism straight, without ice cube or aspirin. At least one of their newspapers has referred to it sneeringly as "lyricism" and has quoted a disparaging comment equating "Senegalese socialism" with "Senegalese mathematics." In the free world, however, where ideas can be discussed with less fanaticism and where truth does not wear a straitjacket, the concept is more likely to be viewed on its merits. A Danish Social Democrat, Jorgen Schleimann, reports on the African socialism seminar held in Dakar in December, 1962, and attended by delegates from sixteen African states: "It would be better," he suggests, "for the world to accept the idea that Africa intends to be socialistic, that in this postcolonial era, Africa is socialistic by its own volition and according to its best precolonial

---

* "Men and nations, however, are often moved not by what is true but by what they *believe* to be true," said Senator J. W. Fulbright in a lecture at the Fletcher School of Law and Diplomacy in April, 1963. "In this sense, it is not Communism that challenges the free world but the misconceptions which Communism fosters, of which the most dangerous is its claim to universal validity. The task of Western policy, therefore, is . . . to demonstrate the futility and danger of its misconceptions, while our major energies are dedicated to the strengthening and improvement of our own society."

traditions. . . . The Africans do not only want socialism; they want an *African* socialism." After summarizing the proceedings of the conference, Mr. Schleimann expresses his firm conviction "that Africa is already getting along fairly well politically, as compared with the rest of the world, and in terms of socialism."*

Other discussions of African socialism have taken place in Europe and America, where Africanists and economists have analyzed the theories and practices of the emergent African nations. As the various experiments in African socialism run their course, and as the literature on the subject becomes increasingly voluminous and controversial, it will be helpful to refer occasionally to this basic, scholarly, and frank blueprint by one of the foremost intellectuals in Africa.

Léopold Sédar Senghor was born in Joal, Senegal, on October 6, 1906, the son of a Peul mother and a prosperous Serer trader. As one of some two dozen brothers and sisters, and as a Catholic in a predominantly Moslem country, young Sédar soon learned the importance of tolerance, of getting along with others. Moreover, in rural Joal, bordering on the bush and on the Atlantic, he gained an early appreciation of the beauty of Senegal, the admirable qualities of the African peasant, the poetry of his folklore, the traditional values of *Négritude*.

His formal studies began nearby at the Catholic Mission of St. Joseph de N'Gasobil, continued at Libermann College and the Dakar *lycée,* and finally took him to Paris and the Lycée Louis le Grand and the Sorbonne. As an *agrégé*—the first Black African to attain that academic distinction—he taught in French secondary schools and at the Ecole Nationale de la France d'Outre-Mer.

Among other things, his student days in Paris broadened his perspective of the Negro world.† Here he formed lifelong

---

* *Preuves-Informations,* April 23, 1963.

† On April 20, 1961, President Senghor told an audience at the Paris City Hall, "If Paris is not the greatest museum of Negro-African art, nowhere else has Negro art been so well understood, commented on, exalted, assimilated. By revealing to me the values of my ancestral civilization, Paris forced me to adopt them and make them bear fruit. Not only me, but a whole generation of Negro students, West Indians as well as Africans."

friendships with French West Indians such as René Maran (whose *Batouala* had won the Goncourt Prize in 1921), Louis T. Achille (who had taught at Howard University and acquired firsthand knowledge of American Negro life and literature), Mlle. Paulette Nardal (Achille's talented cousin, whose salon was a meeting place for literary Negroes and the birthplace of a short-lived periodical), Aimé Césaire (Martinique's brilliant poet and deputy), and Léon G. Damas (Guianan poet and anthologist). Referring to Senghor's reading habits during those early days, Guibert writes, "Not only did he read everything general that appeared, from Proust to Virginia Woolf, from Rilke to Super-vielle, but also all the books about Africa, starting with Frobenius' great work, and the poems of American Negroes."* Personal contacts with Negroes from the Americas complemented Senghor's extensive reading and deepened his respect for the African heritage and his faith in the black man's future. But he never envisioned that future other than as a part of a world civilization where blacks, freed from oppression, and whites, freed from prejudice, could cooperate.

During the war, Senghor was imprisoned by the Nazis. In 1945, General de Gaulle appointed him to the Commission on Colonial Representation in the French Constituent Assembly. One year later, he was elected by Senegal to the French National Assembly, a mandate that was renewed in 1951 and again in 1956. He served as a minister in the third Edgar Faure government and, in July, 1959, was named one of the ministers of the Senate of the French Community. In December, 1959, as President of the National Assembly of the Federation of Mali—a union of Senegal and the Sudanese Republic—he made his masterful and successful plea to De Gaulle for independence. When the Federation dissolved the following August, he was elected President of the Republic of Senegal. In a speech of September 6, 1960, thanking the Senegalese people for the honor and for their confidence, he referred to "Senegalese independence as a prelimi-

* *Op. cit.*, p. 25. Through the years, Senghor has translated American Negro poetry. He also lectured on the subject, and the manuscript of that lecture, along with quite a few of the translations, is to be published in Paris in 1964 in a three-volume edition of Senghor's collected works.

xiv   INTRODUCTION

nary to African cooperation" and even then expressed his willingness to consider "a flexible association" with "our brothers across the Falémé."* He spoke of Senegal as "a link between the Black World and the Arab World," and "a link between Europe and Africa. For, if we have become acclimated here, in 300 years, to the culture and humanism of the West, primarily to that of France, we have also, for the past 15 years, grafted European socialism on to the old roots of Negro-African communalism—I mean, *Négritude*."

In December, 1962, another major crisis confronted Senghor and the Senegalese, in the form of an attempted *coup d'état*. Once again, danger was averted without bloodshed—a tribute to the loyalty, discipline, and political maturity of the Senegalese soldiers and public, and to the statesmanship of Senghor and other national leaders. A few months later, Senegal again proved its attachment to civilized procedures when Ambassador Ousmane Socé Diop ably presented its case against "Portuguese" Guinea before the United Nations Security Council.

Though his heavy responsibilities as Chief of State have understandably interrupted Senghor's preparation of his great work on Negro-African civilization, they have not appreciably curtailed his literary activities. During the first three years of his political stewardship, he wrote monographs on Pierre Teilhard de Chardin, Gaston Berger, and St. John Perse; an article on "West Africa in Evolution" for *Foreign Affairs* (January, 1961); and his essay on Senegalese socialism.† For his fifth volume of verse, *Nocturnes,* he was awarded the International Poetry Prize in 1962.‡ Honor-

* After prolonged negotiation, reconciliation between the Mali Republic and Senegal was finally achieved—dramatically symbolized at the Addis Ababa Conference of 1963, when Presidents Keita and Senghor embraced publicly.

† The third essay in this volume. The first two, written just prior to Senegalese independence, were first published by Présence Africaine in Paris; an abridged American translation of the first essay, under the title *African Socialism,* was published in 1959 by the American Society of African Culture.

‡ His earlier volumes include: *Chants d'ombres* (Paris: Editions du Seuil, 1945); *Hosties noires* (Paris: Editions du Seuil, 1948); *Chants pour Naett* (Paris, Seghers, 1949); and *Ethiopiques* (Paris: Editions du Seuil, 1956). To these we should add his classic *Anthologie de la nouvelle poésie nègre et malgache de langue française* (Paris: Presses Universitaires de France, 1948).

ary doctorates from Fordham, Oxford, and the University of
Paris have accorded recognition of his achievements while en-
hancing the prestige of his race, country, and continent.

Throughout the essays, Senghor stresses the importance of culture in the task of nation-building. He is delighted to report,
for example, that a labor leader in East Germany feels the need
for good literature, or that Russians are reading a novel entitled
Not by Bread Alone. "Contrary to the notion of numerous
African politicians," he observes, "culture is not an appendage
than can be lopped off without damage. It is not even a simple
political means. . . . Culture is inside and outside, above and
beneath all human activities; it is the spirit that animates them,
that gives a civilization its unique style." So much for the theory.
In actual practice, Senghor was one of the earliest collaborators
of his brilliant compatriot Alioune Diop in founding Présence
Africaine in 1947 and the Société Africaine de Culture ten years
later. Senegal is now planning an international festival of Negro-
African art to be held in Dakar in 1965.

In the early 1940's, while Senegal was a colony under the
Vichy Government, we feared that the Nazis might step in and
assume direct control in Western Africa. Journalists reminded
us that only 1,900 miles separate Dakar from Brazil. Today the
destinies of a free Senegal are presided over by a patriot, a states-
man, and a scholar. His program, as described in these three
essays, offers his nation democracy, peace, and progress, not on
the proverbial silver platter, but through persistent, intelligent,
and concerted effort. "Something new out of Africa," it deserves
the sympathetic understanding of those in the free—and the less
free—world who believe in human brotherhood and a more
abundant, meaningful life for all men.

—MERCER COOK

August, 1963

Contents

ON
AFRICAN
SOCIALISM

Author's Foreword

The present volume is an attempt to define an "African road to socialism," built on national values and starting from national realities. The book comprises: (1) the "Report on the Doctrine and Program of the Party," which I made to the Constitutive Congress of the Party of African Federation (PFA) on July 1, 1959; (2) the lecture on "The African Road to Socialism," which I delivered at the first PFA Youth Seminar, in May, 1960; and (3) my lecture of December, 1962, to the Seminar of the Senegalese Progressive Union (UPS) on "The Theory and Practice of Senegalese Socialism."

African political parties in the former "French territories" began, immediately after the liberation of France, to affiliate or even integrate with metropolitan parties. This was natural: Africans needed support in the French parliament; they lacked political experience; they lived in a climate of assimilation. Gradually, however, they realized that no support could be entirely disinterested and that, as protégés, they were at the same time pawns on the chessboard of the French parliamentary game. They learned that all the French political parties, even those on the Left, were national parties formed by national realities and oriented toward national interests. And they discovered that the French proletariat indirectly benefited from colonial exploitation.

From this discovery, combined with the spectacle of the "great events that shook the world," the nationalist feeling was born among colonized people. I was about to forget the powerful leaven furnished Black Africa by the discovery and exaltation of *Négritude,* of Negro-African cultural values. One by one, the African parties drew away from the metropolitan parties. Affiliation replaced integration, and temporary coalition replaced affiliation when independence was not possible in the regular, prescribed manner. No, the metropolitan French could not understand overseas realities—neither the situation nor the needs nor the values of Negro Africans and Malagasy. Even when they did understand, they could not sacrifice the interests of the metropole to those of the overseas territories. To only the best of the French, and especially to General de Gaulle, belongs the honor of having had a perspective on the future, of having understood that these two groups of interests were not hostile but complementary.

We still had not reached 1958. While waiting for France to decolonize, at least in Black Africa, we ourselves had begun to think out our situation in order to provide constructive solutions.* Senegalese politicians left the French Socialist Party in 1948. Their grievance, which transcended personalities—we did not question Guy Mollet's integrity—was that French socialism (like Communism, by the way), not understanding our problems, wanted to apply to Africa a schema made by and for Europe. Thus, to analyze and transform *our* realities, we had to work to define, if not a doctrine, at least an original political method. Year after year, from one political rally to another, by successive stages, alone or in an African movement—the Overseas Independents, the African Convention, the Party of African Federation—we defined our method and program. Other movements, such as the African Democratic Rally (RDA), were performing a similar task.

The three texts presented here represent results of our search. We are, to be sure, Negro Africans mixed with Berbers, born on a certain soil and in a certain climate, with an original cultural heritage. But we are men of the twentieth century, fashioned, whether we like it or not, by a socializing civilization that is

---

* In all fairness, we must admit that Mendès-France had tackled the Indochinese and North African problems; Edgar Faure, the North African and Negro-African problems; and Guy Mollet, the Negro-African problems.

destined to become planetary, as Teilhard de Chardin has observed. In the final analysis, our task is to realize a symbiosis of our Negro-African (or, more precisely, Negro-Berber) values and European values—European values because Europe contributes the principal technical means of the emerging civilization. Not all the values from either side are to be retained: Some are negative; others, belonging to the past, are interesting only as folklore. In a word, sub-Saharan man must realize his full potential as a man of the twentieth century, and at the same time make his contribution to the Civilization of the Universal.

Some may consider this book outdated, since the first two lectures were addressed primarily to Malians and referred to the Mali Federation. But I do not think it is. In addition to its historical interest, the two problems that it treats—nationhood and African socialism—are at the very crux of our African situation. Whether the nation-state be unitary or federal, it will have to resolve these two problems if it wants to exist and to develop.

The fact remains that I was mistaken, we were mistaken, in regard to both the men and the Federation. This is an invitation to modesty that we readily accept from the facts. If we were right to defend the principles of independence in 1958 at the Consultative Constitutional Committee, and to claim effective independence in 1959, we were naïve to believe that a federation was possible in 1959 between states that had been disunited in 1957. We underestimated the present strength of territorialism, of micro-nationalism in Africa. We forgot to analyze and understand the sociological differences among the territories of what used to be French West Africa, differences that the colonial administration had reinforced. This takes priority over personal ambition and the nations' race to leadership.

Does this mean that an ill wind blows nobody any good, and that we must abandon any idea of regroupment or of African unity? I do not think so. Let us simply meditate over the lesson, to become more modest, more prudent, more realistic. African unity is not for tomorrow, not even in the form of the United States of Africa, which I once advocated. Let us speak only of union, and try to regroup the independent African states on the basis of regional and cultural affinities. One cannot develop a nation in the narrow framework of its territorial limits. The facts are there that prove it, as are the European, American, and Asian efforts.

Yes, the breakup of the Mali Federation can be beneficial to the extent that it permits a broader union of twelve independent African states, linked by culture and proximity.* With the exception of Madagascar, they are all located in West Africa. The rupture of the Mali Federation can be beneficial, for it forces us to build this new union, not in a few days, on an ideal constitution, but after long analysis, synthesis, and discussion, on a series of treaties and agreements that extend in time.

This volume does not exhaust the problems. Real independence with a harmonious development of all the potentialities is not achieved once and for all, by magic formulas. It is an always unstable equilibrium—as the Senegalese Gaston Berger† remarked —a never-ending search, a task that is never completed. I have tried, here, to bring my contribution to it.

* This was the Union of African States and Madagascar, formed in Dakar in January, 1961. Known informally as the Brazzaville Powers (after the site of an earlier conference), this Union included the Congo (Brazzaville), Ivory Coast, Senegal, Mauritania, Upper Volta, Niger, Dahomey, Chad, Gabon, Central African Republic, Cameroon, and Madagascar. In May, 1961, these twelve states joined with Liberia, Nigeria, Somalia, Sierra Leone, Togo, Ethiopia, and Libya in the so-called Monrovia Group. [TRANS.]

† The late Gaston Berger (1896–1960), distinguished philosopher and former Director of Higher Education in France, was born in St. Louis du Sénégal. His grandmother was Fatou Diagne of that city. [TRANS.]

Nationhood: Report on the Doctrine and Program of the Party of African Federation*

The Party of African Federation (PFA) was formed, as you know, after the Conference of African Federalists, which met in Dakar on March 24, 1959. This conference marked the culmination of a long effort to regroup African parties. It followed two meetings that were held in Paris, first on February 16–17, then on July 18, 1958. At those different meetings, we compared our respective programs in order to retain their basic principles—not what divided us, but what united us over and beyond the particular interests of men and states. What unites us is a common resolve to build step by step a federal State, better still, a Negro-African nation, freely associated with France in a confederation.

Only those who had betrayed the program of Bamako (1957) and Cotonou (1958) were absent from those meetings. For the Bamako Conference, far from rejecting basic federation, had expressly advocated "the democratization of federal executives." What else could this mean but the replacement of the High Commissioner by a federal government elected by a federal assembly? Moreover, Houphouët-Boigny, President of the RDA,

* *Report to the Constitutive Congress of the PFA, July 1, 1959.*

7

had advanced this interpretation in his address to the RDA territorial affiliates. As for the Cotonou Conference, it assigned as the
ultimate aim of the Party of African Regroupment (PRA) the
realization of a multinational confederation with France. But its
general political resolution recommended the formation of "a
solid, progressive, African community prior to the free, egalitarian political cooperation with any other community."

Before proceeding, let us have the courage to criticize ourselves.
To effect a compromise, when it was really too late for compromise, some of us were too timid at Bamako, others were too
adventurous at Cotonou. Today, with cool head and clear eyes,
we shall analyze our situation, which has already changed from
that of last year, in order to suggest solutions that are both fair
and constructive. We shall avoid two dangers: opportunism,
which is excessive submissiveness to the facts, and verbalism,
which believes in the effectiveness of slogans. Facts are transitory;
they must be placed in their historic context and interpreted
dynamically. Slogans are simplifiers; they distort reality, substi-
tuting analogous representations even though the situations are
never identical.

For several years, we have talked much of independence. True
independence is that of the spirit. A people is not really independent when, after its accession to nominal independence, its
leaders import, without modification, institutions—political, economic, social, or cultural—that are the natural fruits of the geography and history of another race. I do not deny that every
institution, every moral or technical value, is related to man, and
thus has some universal validity. Nevertheless, it must be adapted
to the realities of the native soil, by retaining the spirit rather
than the form. We would impoverish ourselves and probably
despair of reducing our age-old backwardness as compared with
Europe if, on the pretext of anticolonialist struggle, we refuse
Europe's contributions. In the words of the Tunisian labor leader,
Ahmed Ben Salah:

> At the risk of retrogressing, decolonization must not be the inverse
> of colonization. The failure of several formerly colonized countries
> can only be attributed to this superficial, negative, and sterile formal-
> ism. Decolonization must first entail a profound revolution of mental,

moral, social, and economic structures. This revolution is not destruction of the colonial contribution, but utilization and fundamental reorientation of it, considered as a tool snatched from colonization and susceptible of serving a new purpose.[1]

Paraphrasing a leader of the Istiqlal, I would summarize: "It is a question not of destroying but of transcending the colonial fact."*

Independence is not a refusal, it is a choice: a choice of goal and of means, as a function of our present situation. We are not in the same situation as our ancestors, even less in that of the founders of the old Mali Empire. Since their time, there has been the colonial fact, with the ensuing dependence in interdependence. There have been two world wars and all their consequences. There has been the Constitution of October 4, 1958. And, above all, there was in 1959 the possibility of a free choice. It is now a matter of selecting, among European methods, the most effective ones for an exact analysis of our situation. It is a question of borrowing those of its institutions, values, and techniques that are most likely to fecundate our traditional civilization. I say "our civilization," for we shall not be building from scratch. To do so would surely be to head for failure, for there is no *tabula rasa*. We shall retain whatever should be retained of our institutions, our techniques, our values, even our methods. From all this—African acquisitions and European contributions—we shall make a dynamic symbiosis to fit Africa and the twentieth century, but first of all to fit Man. Already you recognize the socialist method. Independence is there, and not elsewhere.

I. The Will to Nationhood

If the congress of the League of Communists, held in London in November, 1847, was, with the publication of the *Communist Manifesto,* the most significant event in the nineteenth century, the Bandung Conference of 1955 can undoubtedly be considered its counterpart in the twentieth century. Analysis reveals a sim-

* The Istiqlal, Party of Moroccan Independence, formed during World War II, is still the leading political party of that country. [TRANS.]

ilar alienation in both instances. The proletariat of the nine-teenth century was estranged from humanity; the colonized peo-ple of the twentieth century, the colored peoples, are estranged even more seriously. To economic alienations, others are added: political, social, and cultural. The result is physical and moral suffering, poverty, and uneasy conscience, the latter stemming from a feeling of frustration. In both instances, revolt and strug-gle serve to "abolish present conditions" and "transform the world" by re-establishing the natural equilibrium. Where colored peoples are concerned, it is accurate to speak of a "revolt against the West."

However, since the situations are not identical, although sim-ilar, the aims of the revolutions are not exactly the same. In Europe, it is a question of eliminating inequalities arising from the formation of classes. In Africa, it is a question of eliminating inequalities arising from the colonial conquest, from political domination.

Though we must start from our situation, from our alienation, it would not be fair to insist on it, although its aftereffects are still present. For the situation as we have just briefly analyzed it no longer really exists. It has already been rendered *passé* by the Constitution of 1958. We are now fully autonomous and more than autonomous. We have freedom to choose.

Nation, Fatherland, State

And we have chosen. The PFA made its choice on March 24, 1959. Its objective is the achievement of a French-speaking, Negro-African nation, of which the federal state, the Federation of Mali, constitutes the first step. This is our opportunity to answer metropolitan Frenchmen who deny that the Mali Federa-tion can be a state. In the Littré dictionary of 1956 one reads on page 1097: "State: . . . the government, supreme administration of a country." The Federation of Mali is therefore a state since it has its own government and administration. We may add that it also has its own parliament and judicial system. We read in the same Littré, on page 1460: "Federation: a political union of states. The American Federation." No commentary is necessary.

Mali is at once a state and a federation, since Senegal and Sudan are federated states. The least that can be expected of Frenchmen is that they respect the French language and French law as we do. It is not permissible that they concoct a trumped-up quarrel* with us.

At this point it is appropriate to distinguish between *Nation* and *State*. First we shall note the difference between *Nation* and *Fatherland*. The idea of Nation, in the modern sense of the term, was developed in France during the seventeenth and eighteenth centuries. It found its purest expression during the Revolution of 1789. As Denis de Rougemont pertinently observes in an article entitled "Fédéralisme et Nationalisme,"[2] the French soldiers at Valmy did not shout "Long live France!" or "Long live the Fatherland!" but "Long live the Nation!" What does this mean?

The fatherland is the heritage handed down to us by our ancestors: a land, a blood, a language or at least a dialect, mores, customs, folklore, art—in a word, a culture rooted in a native soil and expressed by a race. In old France, one's fatherland was identified with one's province. This idea was what the Girondins, who were federalists, wished to maintain. In West Africa, the fatherland is the Serer country, the Malinké country, the Songhai country, the Mossi, the Baoulé, or the Fon.

The nation groups such fatherlands together in order to transcend them. Unlike them, it is not a natural determination and therefore an expression of the milieu, but a conscious will to construct or reconstruct. Objectively, it is a *re-structuration* along the lines of an exemplary model or archetype. But to attain its objective, the nation must inspire all its members, all individuals, with faith in nationhood over and above the fatherlands. It must make persons out of individuals—in other words, it must make conscious wills, *souls*. Far from rejecting the realities of the fatherland, the nation will lean on them, or, more precisely, will lean on their virtues, on their quality of immediate reality, on their emotional strength. It will unite these virtues of the fatherlands; most often, it will choose those virtues which, by reason

* *Une querelle d'allemand* in the French: literally, "a German quarrel." [TRANS.]

of climate, history, or race, share a common denominator or a universal value. Once achieved, the nation forges a harmonious ensemble out of its different provinces: a single country for a single people, animated by one faith and striving toward the same goal. In the words of Hegel, the theoretician of the nation-state: "It is not the natural limits of the nation that form its character, but rather its national spirit."

As can be inferred, the nation is superior to the fatherland on the level of humanity, and even in term of efficiency. It distills the values of the latter, sublimates them by transcending them. In this respect, it is *humanization*. For the proper characteristic of Man is to snatch himself from the earth, to rise above his roots and blossom in the sun, to escape in an act of *freedom* from his "natural determinations." It is by liberty that man conquers nature and reconstructs it on a universal scale, that man realizes himself as a god; this is freedom.

If the nation is a conscious determination to reconstruct, the state is its major means. The state is to the nation what the contractor is to the architect. It is incarnate in the institutions: government, parliament, public services. The government officials are its workers. It fulfills the nation's will and ensures its permanence. In domestic affairs, it mingles the fatherlands and shapes the individuals into the mold of the archetype. In external affairs, it defends the nation's integrity and preserves it from foreign intrigues. The two temptations of the state are *assimilation* and *imperialism,* for it is by nature a conqueror. We shall see later on how we can be inoculated against these diseases of the state.

The Federation

The delegates to the Constituent Assembly of the Mali Federation of January 17, 1959, were wise to proceed by stages. A nation is not realized in a day; like fruit, it needs an inner ripening. The building of a state resembles that of a cathedral in the Middle Ages. It is a long-term enterprise, requiring centuries of effort and patience. It took France nearly 2,000 years—up to Napoleon's time—to become a nation-state, and she was the first in Europe to do so.

We were wise to begin at the beginning, with the foundation, with a federation of states, the Mali Federation. This did not suppress the federated republics; it simply coordinated their policies by transferring to the federal authorities only the general prerogatives, strictly defined and limited. We must await the adherence of the other states of former French West Africa to see in what direction and how far we shall go. We must also test the results of the first phase by experience. The fact remains that the Mali Federation is a state, with its own government, parliament, system of justice, and administrative services. It has authority to sign agreements with other member states of the Community, except the French Republic. Mali provides the basis for a Negro-African nation, with a flag, an anthem, and a motto.

I personally do not believe that it will ever be necessary to form a unitary state. The most powerful nations today are federal states: the United States, the Soviet Union, China, India, Canada, and Brazil. The weakness of France comes perhaps from her excessive centralization, a weakness that most clear-sighted Frenchmen are now beginning to recognize. All that could be done would be to effect a redistribution, a new cutting up of the federated states. You can imagine what psychological difficulties such a procedure would encounter, because of the crystallizations —the routines and prejudices—already in existence. Men cannot be handled like piles of dead wood. Above all else, we shall take care not to succumb to one of the temptations of the nation-state: the uniformization of people across fatherlands. The archetype is the impoverishment of persons, their reduction to the status of robot-individuals, their loss of vitality and sap.

Wealth springs from the diversities of countries and persons, from the fact that they complement each other. We shall always remember a truth often expressed by Father Teilhard de Chardin: Races are not equal but complementary, which is a superior form of equality. Whence the superiority of the federal over the unitary state. I shall go even further. There is but one way to reduce the tyranny of the state, to ward off its diseases, as the socialist Proudhon said, and that way is through federalism—in other words, the decentralization and deconcentration of its economic and political institutions.

We can regret that Dahomey did not join the Mali Federation
and that Upper Volta did not remain a member.* But on second
thought, their choices were fortunate from both the political and
the economic point of view. In contrast to their constituents,
the prime ministers of those two states were never federalists by
conviction. In the Federation of Mali they would have caused
dissention, or, at the very least, they would have strained the
federal links.

We have made a good start in Mali by uniting populations
whose natural characteristics—climate, soil, blood, language and
customs, art and literature—are similar. Senegal and Sudan constitute, what is more, a rather homogeneous and relatively rich
economic unit. In the old French West Africa, these two alone
furnished almost half the revenue of the entire territory. With
the best harbor [Dakar], the most powerful industrial set-up, and
a market of 7 million consumers, we have important advantages.
I note in passing that many of the African government employees
and technicians in our upper cadres are not originally from Mali.
The freedom enjoyed here represents another asset.

And yet, in the interest of Black Africa and of France, our aim
must be to unite within the Mali Federation all the states of
former French West Africa and to sign, in the meantime, economic and cultural pacts with other states, including the Republic of Guinea. By so doing, we shall only be following the
French example.

The principal and permanent objective of the kings of France
for nearly a thousand years was to make a *nation* out of diverse
races and to extend their kingdom to the natural frontiers of
ancient Gaul. These frontiers were natural, however, only in the
geographical and economic sense; to the anthropologist, the
Basque differs more from the Fleming or Breton than the Wolof
differs from the Baoulé or Fon. The aim was progressively to
reduce the provincial fatherlands and assimilate them into the
Ile de France, which imposed its dialect as the national language.

---

* The first announcement of the Mali Federation said it would include
Senegal, Sudan, Upper Volta, and Dahomey. Referendums in the latter two
states defeated the proposal, and later, both Upper Volta and Dahomey associated with Niger and the Ivory Coast in the *Conseil de l'Entente*. [Trans.]

In West Africa, if we may limit ourselves to this example, France borrowed, for her own use, the great design of the emperors of Mali and Songhai: to link Senegal to the Hausa country and the Sahara oases to the Gulf of Benin, in order to group the "Sudanese" races into an economically and politically viable entity. Our intention is not different. Why should what was good for France and Black Africa in the first half of the twentieth century no longer be so in the second half? Could logic have ceased to be French, and common sense Negro-African?

The reconstruction of the old French West African federation on new bases is in the political interest of the Africans; it is clearly in line with our concept of "Nation." Upper Volta and Niger are grassland, prairie countries, like Senegal and Sudan. The fact that the Ivory Coast and Dahomey are composed mostly of forests offers an additional reason for not separating them from the other countries. They are *complementary,* necessary to the others as the others are necessary to them.

The reconstruction of the old federation is also in the political interest of France; this is obvious to anyone who follows the extension of the Cold War to Black Africa. Guinea provides a typical example, as does—we dare say—the Ghana-Guinea Union. The Cold War is being waged not only between East and West, but also secretly among the members of NATO. (We know that the British Foreign Office did not look with disfavor on the birth of this union.) We can be sure that the French-speaking states, troubled by domestic difficulties, run the risk of swinging, one by one, toward the Commonwealth or the people's democracies. What can Dahomey do, situated between Nigeria and Ghana? How can the poverty-stricken people of Niger resist the attraction of a rich and democratic Nigeria, inhabited, moreover, by 35 million people?

The reconstruction of the old federation is, finally, in the interest of the French Community. I have often said that the association of the earthenware pot and the iron pot is contrary to nature; based on unequal strength, it causes trouble, engenders weakness. However, the strength of each partner is moral as well as material, political as well as economic. The French Community will be strong only to the extent that the states—I mean their populations—feel that they are morally equal partners with a real share in the decisions of the Community's Executive Council. How could this be achieved if they came to it disunited, while the metropolitan French ministers of the Community formed a cohesive bloc? How could this be achieved if they had the discouraging impression that their progress depended not on their united organizational effort, but rather on the pleasure of metropolitan France?

More than the awareness of their poverty, it was just such a feeling of frustration, their inferiority complex, that pushed the peoples of Bandung toward revolt against the privileged nations, against the West. We fear that the *balkanization* of Black Africa, unless remedied, may lead to a new Bandung for the French Community. And we know that the most formidable revolts are not effected by men with guns in their hands, but by men whose arms are folded in passive resistance.

The Federation offers an economic as well as a political advantage. Economists have claimed repeatedly that *development* requires extension of the domestic market, in addition to the accumulation of capital. This is where the basic material power of the Big Two lies. For example, the domestic trade of the United States is ten times the volume of its foreign commerce. This obvious truth also explains the creation of the European Common Market. The largest nations of the EEC have populations of 45–60 million and an annual per capita income twice that of former French West Africa, with a population of only about 20 million. How, then, can one believe that the erection of eight customs barriers would aid our development? Our industrialists have admitted that, if the balkanization of French-speaking Black Africa is maintained, they will be compelled to close their factories. For the first quarter of 1959, customs and fiscal income on imports was already down 12 per cent. No lyricism, no sentimentality can refute these facts.

The eight states of the former French West Africa stand to lose economically from balkanization. France likewise. As I have stated elsewhere, experts estimate that, unless the common market of the former French West Africa is re-established, France will have to provide—in addition to the credits allotted by the

Fund for Aid and Cooperation—7 billion CFA* francs to balance the budgets of the poorer states.

The antifederalist states are beginning to acknowledge these facts. Willingly or unwillingly, they are led to regroup, to form a federation or federations, indirectly. An article published by Philippe Decraene in *Le Monde* of May 5, 1959, is significant in this connection:

> Without renouncing the doctrinal positions that he has been defending since the Bamako Conference of October, 1957, Houphouët-Boigny has just decided to set up, *under the leadership of the Ivory Coast,* a territorial regrouping comprising Upper Volta, Niger, and perhaps, later, Dahomey. Rejecting any formula of a "super-government" or "super-ministry," this project places economic collaboration and administrative coordination ahead of political preoccupations. At any rate, its promoter denies that it has any federal aspect *in the strict sense.* Despite its different character, this regrouping is, in fact, parallel to the Mali Federation. It will modify considerably *the equilibrium of political forces* in former French West Africa, and will not insist, as the promoters of the Mali Federation are now doing, on the theme of eventual independence [Italics mine].

One could not express this better—all the more so because *Le Monde* is not noted as a pro-Mali newspaper.

Those lines merit reflection. If the new grouping is to "modify the equilibrium of political forces in former French West Africa," this proves that, beyond economic preoccupations, the intention is to set up a political operation. The introductory sentence to Decraene's article said: "Before the meeting of the Executive Council, the heads of RDA governments met at Houphouët-Boigny's residence to compare points of view and to harmonize their attitudes on matters treated by the Council on Monday afternoon." What were they doing "in that boat" if not something political? Despite his sympathies for the RDA, Decraene found it difficult to refrain from seeing in the projected regrouping a political institution, the beginning of a federation. How

---

* The value of a CFA, or West African, franc is twice that of a metropolitan franc. Thus, the rate of exchange for CFA francs is approximately 245 to the dollar. [TRANS.]

fortunate the French language is, how fertile in subtleties, where understatement says "least" when it means "most"!

That is the disguised federation which is being formed to oppose Mali. Its weakness will lie in not being a "federation in the strict sense" but an instrument at the service of a state. As we are warned, the new grouping will be effected "under the leadership of the Ivory Coast." I have nothing against the Ivory Coast—we must avoid any bitterness against her and consider her a sister state. I do not underestimate her agricultural potentialities; I affirm that she is the greatest Negro-African art center. But I simply state one additional fact: As the richest state, the Ivory Coast will seize not only political hegemony, but also the lion's share in the economic sector. She will gain an important market for her industries at little expense. She will retain for herself the major portion of the customs receipts and fiscal taxes on imports, leaving France the task of meeting the budgetary deficit of the poor states. The other weakness of this *Entente* will be in its reliance more on French generosity, on a policy of facility, than on a policy of rigor and austerity. A nation, and a state even less, is not built on policies of facility but by labor, by the conscious effort of all its citizens. In any event, it does not advance the cause of African unity to make—with the help of certain politicians in Paris—Dahomey and Upper Volta leave the Mali Federation so as to create a new group in opposition to it.

As you know, the Mali Federation rests on quite different bases, first of all, on honesty. The *Entente* "will not insist," Decraene announced, "as the promoters of the Mali Federation are now doing, on the theme of eventual independence." That we are doing so is first proof of our frankness. We do not have one language for Europeans and another for Africans. We do not say to the former, "There is no longer any political problem between France and Africa; we renounce independence forever." And to the latter, "Let us ask France for massive aid and, when we are ready, we shall take our independence." Let us say that even in politics honesty is the best policy. The greatest cleverness often consists in not being clever at all.

In the Federation of Mali, however, the important thing is that there is no leader-state, but complete solidarity among the

member states. In other words, the only leadership belongs to the
Federation, to the general interest. Customs receipts and taxes
on imports go first to the federal services. The balance is shared
by the federated states according to their needs, it being understood that the fiscal effort and the austerity effort will everywhere
be the same.

As for the permanent secretariat created to administer common services in the former French Equatorial Africa, it has the
advantage over the *Entente* of being set up on an egalitarian
basis. But its weakness is that it entrusts to technicians those
powers that normally belong to politicians. The death of that
strong personality, our friend Barthélémy Boganda, may prevent
the permanent secretariat from paving the way for a real federation.

Our conclusion concerning the Federation is that it will serve
the best interests of the whole French Community. The British
and Belgians, who are realists, have understood the problem more
clearly, I regret to say. It is true that the Africans themselves are
primarily responsible for the balkanization. The British accepted
Nigerian independence only on condition that the Federation be
safeguarded. As for the Belgians, a recent speech by Van Hemel-
rijck, Minister to the Congo and Ruanda-Urundi, leaves no doubt
as to their intentions: to lead the Congo gradually to independence, but in unity. At any rate, balkanization will be avoided,
even against the will of the Congolese. Both the British and
Belgians intend to fulfill, to the end, their duties as guardians
and not allow their wards to dissipate the family heritage.

The Community

Those of us who have carefully read the French Constitution
of October 4, 1958, and those who attentively observe the establishment of the institutions of the Community, will frankly agree
that these answer our grievances and hopes.

One need only read a few constitutions of federal states—those
of Canada, India, the United States, the German Federal Republic—to perceive that we in Black Africa have obtained complete domestic autonomy, and more. Indeed, the status of our

republics is mid-way between autonomy and independence; the status of the Community is between that of a federation and a confederation. In a classic federation, the number of matters shared in common may be as many as thirty. According to the Constitution of October 4, there are not necessarily more than five of these. This is not a negligible detail. Moreover, the last line of Article 78 anticipates that "special agreements may establish other common fields of competence or provide for any transfer of competence from the Community to one of its members." One does not need to be a sorcerer to foresee that the latter eventuality will always occur. Above all, there are Articles 86 and 88. Article 86 permits any member state to "become independent." This requires a simple "resolution of the legislative assembly of the State concerned, approved," it is true, "by a local referendum, organized and supervised by the institutions of the Community." This is normal. But I fail to see how the Community—to which we belong—could resist a popular upsurge. As for the agreement that will legally sanction the referendum provided it is "approved by the Parliament of the Republic" and "the legislative assembly concerned," this agreement, despite what has been said in certain African circles, does not concern the principle but only the means of applying independence. That, too, is normal. Though they have acquired independence, Morocco and Tunisia have nonetheless signed agreements for the transfer of authority. And this process has not yet terminated. Article 88 permits states that have become independent to sign pacts of association with the French Republic or with the Community.

As a matter of fact, we are *independent* in the etymological sense of the word. As we have said, independence is essentially nondependence in one's decisions: *freedom to choose*. We were free to choose on September 28, 1958.* We are still, at any moment, free to choose the road to our destiny. We would be ungrateful not to recognize this fundamental freedom which is ours.

Let us continue our analysis of the concept of independence.

* The referendum of September 28, 1958, allowed French overseas territories to decide by voting *oui* or *non,* whether or not to remain in the French Community. [TRANS.]

Our first observation is that, like any concept, it does not embrace all reality, but simplifies it dangerously to the extent that it becomes a legal term. For a jurist, independence is a *form,* not a reality. The independent state is one that is so recognized, *de jure,* internationally. To a lesser degree, it is a state that has the external signs of sovereignty: an army and a diplomacy, I do not even say a currency. Now there are armies and armies, diplomacies and diplomacies. Those of the Big Two are really armies and diplomacies. Who would dare affirm that those of a given "dwarf-state" in Asia or Africa really are? In other words, legal independence is indeed *nominal* and not necessarily *real.* A certain African state that acquired its independence 150 years ago continues to vilify colonialism, which proves that it is not yet really independent.

We federalists here assembled were the first to preach African unity and to distinguish between nominal and real independence. Now the antifederalists are borrowing our language. This is a tribute rendered by error to truth. Far from abandoning our theses, we must maintain them by implanting them more deeply. Thus we shall make them effective instruments for understanding and transforming reality.

We shall not say, after the manner of antifederalists reassuring the right-wing metropolitan party, "There is no political problem between France and Black Africa." Instead, we shall say, "The Constitution has defined an effective method for resolving problems that will continue to arise." We shall not say, "We renounce independence forever." Instead, we shall declare, "The Constitution of October 4 allows us to prepare and organize our independence, step by step."

Borrowing a Communist trick, while claiming to be anti-Communist, one could temporarily postpone the problem of independence. But it cannot be eluded. The history of the twentieth century poses it for all the colored peoples. The best method is to face the problem realistically in order to solve it effectively. A nation cannot flower in dependency. The problem is to know what independence is and how to attain it.

A purely nominal independence is a false one. It may satisfy national pride, but it does not eliminate the awareness of alienation, the frustration, and the inferiority complex, since it cannot resolve the concrete problems confronting the underdeveloped countries: housing, clothing, feeding, curing, and educating the masses. We shall accord high priority to the harmonious and rapid development of our underdeveloped countries. As we have seen, the Mali Federation, generally speaking, will be our major agency. But it will be integrated in a larger entity, the Community, and associated with an even larger one, the European Common Market.

As we develop economically and socially, as we train the cadres necessary for the state, and as we raise the standard of living along with the level of education, we shall amicably negotiate with the Community the transfer of authority anticipated in Article 78 of the 1958 Constitution. In the end, we shall possess all the outward indications of sovereignty, of nominal independence. If we prove our capacity for autonomous organization and administration, it is inconceivable that France will refuse to grant us our nominal independence. It will suffice to amend Article 77, replacing "The States enjoy autonomy" by "The States enjoy independence." Let us seek real independence, and the rest will be given to us.*

Does this imply that we should leave the Community to negotiate a pact of association in accordance with Article 88? We think not. Objectively, this would be a poorer solution, for we should be abandoning the substance for the shadow. If we sincerely believe in the need for great intercontinental ensembles, we shall find more advantages in a multinational community than in a loose and inadequately defined association. If we hold firmly to what has always been our common ideal, a multinational confederation, if we prove in concrete action that we envisage the flowering of our destiny within the Community, French opinion will be grateful to us. And we need the support of that opinion for our development. The point is not to sacrifice everything to it, especially not our Negro-African dignity.

* Several months after this *Report* was written, France amended the Constitution of October 4 to permit independent states to remain within the Community, and on June 20, 1960, Senegal achieved complete independence. [TRANS.]

The dynamic evolution of the Community, in line with the inevitable trend of history, is to our advantage. It is also in the interest of France. On the economic level, France can get along without Black Africa, but she cannot get along without it on the political or cultural plane. France is not Holland. She is a great lady who needs to spread her radiance over a large family. Reduced to her European dimensions, she would fail in her mission to the world, which is to defend Man; she would lose her soul and her *raison d'être*.

If France could only understand that, she would understand not only the Negro Africans, but also the Arab-Berbers of North Africa. Then the victory would be hers. With our mutual consent, she would convert the Community into a *Commonwealth à la française*. Independent states, formerly protectorates or colonies, would perhaps agree to enter this Franco-African Confederation. We think that a solution could be found to the Algerian problem in this perspective, that cancer gnawing at the side of France. At any rate, we have a part to play in this situation.

We shall participate loyally in the Community, along the lines already indicated. This imposes duties upon us. First, we must be faithful to our doctrine and program. Then, we must be realistic. We shall be interested in actions more than in words. Fiery speeches are the least effective, for they frighten but do not persuade. When sons come of age they find a home; they loosen family ties but do not break them. To a considerable extent, we are the spiritual sons of France.

Our third duty is to remember that only confidence begets confidence. We must continue to trust the people of France and General de Gaulle, President of the Republic and of the Community. I know well that the French have their faults; they also have their qualities. What an admirable and sometimes disappointing people, at once seductive and irritating! They were the first, in Europe, to become a nation; rich in virtues—engineer and soldier, artist and artisan—the people of France are imperialistic, assimilationist, emotional; they are reasonable, realistic, human. They try to impose their ideas and feelings on facts. They prefer their prestige to their interests; they want not so much to be loved as to be told they are loved. But when one presents a solid, factual refutation, they finally bow to the truth —through reason and humanity.

As for General de Gaulle, during the bitter hours of the Nazi occupation, we trusted him to save France from racist dictatorship and, at the same time, to save Black Africa. He did not fail us. How can we blame him for being both obdurate and clever? He is French; the realist in him never lets itself be stifled by the idealist. He is human; above all, he is loyal, with a loyalty that the ultras call weakness. We need only to debate calmly and to present arguments supported by facts.

We shall not silence our conviction that our loyalty requires from France a like loyalty. Not only from General de Gaulle, but also from the political parties and Government of the French Republic. It is inadmissible that certain political parties and ministers have the disagreeable habit of meddling in our elections and in the formation of our governments. The most recent example was that of Dahomey. Significantly, it was the Dahomean section of the General Union of Workers of Black Africa, affiliated with the RDA, that protested against sending a delegation to Paris to resolve the Dahomean crisis.

It is also necessary that the authorities of the Community treat African political parties and states impartially. Yet some of us are now placed to the right of the Father, with the white lambs, while others are relegated to the left, with the goats in the outer darkness. When the Ivory Coast was given the most powerful radio transmitter in the territory, of 25,000 watts, no one protested. Why, then, should the same Ivory Coast and its chorus of satellites object to Mali receiving a transmitter of equal power that will enable us to reach all corners of the Federation?

We must still consider a most important problem: the exercise of civil liberties. Article 77 of the Constitution stipulates: "There exists in the Community only one citizenship. All citizens are equal before the law, whatever their origin, race, or religion. They have the same duties." When certain African states refused to organize elections after voting their new constitutions, and when certain others fabricated *ad hoc* electoral laws, sometimes by decree—the one in Upper Volta is a model—we could answer that these were domestic matters in those states. What is less understandable is that the Community authorities remain undisturbed when a state deports a citizen of the Community without a trial. Soon one will have to be English, American, Russian, or Chinese to enjoy the rights of man in a state of the Community. Mali cannot remain unmoved by the expulsion of its citizens. If it is unable to convince the governments of the antifederalist states, it will have to submit the matter to the Court of Arbitration. If no satisfaction is forthcoming, it could then legitimately take measures of reprisal. Under such circumstances, the Community would obviously have ceased to exist. A house divided against itself cannot stand. Let us hope that matters will not go that far.

II. The Road to Nationhood

We have said that the State is the expression of the Nation; it is primarily a means to achieve the Nation. Political history teaches that the lack of state organization is a weakness that brings on the fatal disintegration of the nation. The history of the Fourth French Republic illustrates this. In the first phase of nation-building, we must organize the public powers of the federal state and of the federated states to provide a structure to guarantee their authority and permanence. We must also define the program that will orient the action of these public powers— governments and parliaments. For only this action can make of our various populations a *People,* that is to say, a *Community,* where each individual will identify himself with the collective whole and vice versa. But the *unanimity,* the *communion* of souls is not enough. For the people to become a nation, the individual must grow as his standard of living and culture is raised. Our Constitution guarantees the strength and stability of the public powers. Our program, inspired by our doctrine, will permit the federal State to realize the *Negro-African Nation.*

At the moment, it is still too early to describe our program in detail. We must first assure a cultural base for the future nation, by defining the essential characteristics of traditional Negro-African civilization which, blending with European and French contributions, will undergo a renaissance. We must also make an objective appraisal of our economic situation—our riches, our deficiencies, our potentials. Only these inventories will enable us to draw up a long-term program, a harmonious development plan of our possibilities. All we intend to do, all we can do today, is to pose the problem. This will not be, as is too often the case at meetings of African political parties, a catalog of grievances or campaign promises, but the definition of a method: the probable course of our development.

Socialism Is a Humanism

In the respective programs of our former parties, all of us used to proclaim our attachment to *socialism*. This was a good thing, but it was not enough. Most of the time, we were satisfied with stereotyped formulas and vague aspirations that we called *scientific socialism*, as if socialism did not mean a return to original sources. Above all, we need to make an effort to rethink the basic texts in the light of Negro-African realities. Let us first consider the main question.

The antifederalists have accused us of being atheists, "Marxists," and of outlawing religion. Surely this smacks of propaganda. Can we integrate Negro-African cultural values, especially religious values, into socialism? We must answer that question once and for all with an unequivocal *yes*.

We are not "Marxists" in the sense given the word today, insofar as Marxism is presented as atheistic metaphysics, a total and totalitarian view of the world, a *Weltanschauung*. Marx himself once said: "As for me, I am not a Marxist." We are *socialists*. In other words, we shall exclude neither Marx nor Engels from our sources; we shall start from their works as from those of the "Utopian socialists," and we shall add to these sources the works of their successors and commentators. But we shall retain only the method and the ideas: the method, to help us to analyze our situation; the ideas, to help us to solve our problems.

We shall start from Marx and Engels. Whatever their limitations, their inadequacies, or their errors, they, more than all others, revolutionized the political and economic thought of the nineteenth century. The consequences of that revolution are still perceptible in the twentieth. Churchmen themselves cannot deny Marx's contributions and they accept his positive values. And since the liberation, they have perhaps contributed most to an understanding of Marx—in France, at least. As proof of this, I need cite only two French Marxists. "A final paradox," writes Henri Lefebvre, the "Master Marxist" in France, is that "the most important works on Marxism published recently are signed by Jesuits." And Lucien Goldmann, speaking of these same volumes, notes that they "constitute at the moment the principal French contribution to the study of Marxism."[3] I may particularly draw your attention to Father Bigo's book entitled *Marxisme et Humanisme*. It bears the same title that I gave to an earlier article of my own published in *La Revue socialiste*.[4]

We shall take Marx's ideas, theory, and theories as a starting point. Marx borrows economic concepts and vocabulary from his predecessors. To be sure, he is interested in statistics, which were then in limbo, but he cites facts and figures without verifying or criticizing them. What interests him more than things themselves is man's relationship with other men and with things. He is the real founder of sociology. According to a famous expression, his goal is "to penetrate the real and intimate totality of the relationship of production in bourgeois society." The fact is that Marx came to economics through philosophy, detouring through Hegel, from whom he borrowed the theory of *alienation*, and Feuerbach, who taught him the importance of *praxis*. His sociology is based on the general theory of alienation, which he develops through the particular theories of *value* and *capital*. I shall take the latter as my point of departure.

For Marx, a commodity is the elementary form of wealth in capitalist-type societies, and every commodity has two values: a *use-value* and an *exchange-value*. The use-value of an object is based on human needs; it is "limited by the physical properties of the commodity [and] has no existence apart from that commodity."[5] It is the material support of the exchange-value. In a capitalist economy—that is, in a money-market economy—the exchange-value is substituted for the use-value and becomes the *value* in itself, and "the magnitude of the value of any article is

the amount of labor socially nceessary, or the labor-time socially necessary for its production."[6] This is the *labor* theory of
value. In other words, within a patriarchal, community economy,
commodities born of human needs remain in the hands of men.
In a market economy, these same commodities escape from the
conscious determination of men, are subject to the monetary law
of exchange, and establish objective relationships among themselves. The world of things is substituted for the world of men
and dominates it. Men are cut off from nature and from each
other. They have entered the world of *capital*.

Capital could not be identified with the means of production
themselves. The latter existed just as well in the patriarchal community. Capital is the means of production monopolized by a
minority of men. For Marx, capital is even more than that. It is
an idea that takes life and is personified, a conscious and im-
placable will that becomes incarnate in a monstrous force. It is
money whose final objective is to make money. The objective is
not to satisfy human needs, not even animal needs—food, clothing, shelter—but rather to grab the surplus-value of the worker's
labor. It is here that the theory of *surplus-value* intervenes.

The value of a commodity is here determined by the amount
of labor needed to produce it. This value should normally correspond to the number of hours needed to make this commodity;
in a human economy, it should correspond to the number of
hours necessary to assure the livelihood of the worker and his
family—his material and spiritual life. Let us suppose that this
number of hours is five. The capitalist ought to pay the worker
on the basis of five hours. However, though he pays him on this
basis, he makes him work eight hours, but the value of the three
extra hours goes to the employer and not to the worker. It is this
surplus-value that, according to Marx, permits the "accumulation
of capital," *capitalization*. The employer could object that he has
taken the risk and provided the means of production. The socialist replies that the investment is amortized after a few years,
whereas the surplus-value remains indefinitely. But this is perhaps not the essential argument. Marx's general theory is a
macro-economic one. What he is considering is the totality of

workers and the totality of capitalists, which eliminates the idea of risk.

In the light of these analyses, we can now explain the general theory of *alienation* that underlies them. The theory of alienation is not precisely discussed in *Capital* but rather in the philosophical works of Marx, as well as in a posthumously published manuscript called "Alienated Labour." Without these early works of Marx, it would be difficult to understand *Capital*.

For Marx, man is essentially a *producing artist*. This is what distinguishes him from the animal. Both are placed in nature, better still, both are products of nature—geography and history —and realize their potential only in and through nature, which is given to us at the outset as an inorganic, objective world. The animal does not transform nature; he *naturally* extracts from it his "immediate means of subsistence" in the sense that he is moved by his instinct. He does not aim beyond the satisfaction of his material needs.

If, on the other hand, man realizes himself *in* nature, he does so even more *through* nature. He does not passively submit to the productive forces of nature, he acts on them:

> [Animals] produce only under the compulsion of direct physical needs, while man produces when he is free from physical need and only truly produces in freedom from such need. . . . Animals construct only in accordance with the standards and needs of the species to which they belong, while man knows how to produce in accordance with the standards of every species and knows how to apply the appropriate standard to the object. Thus man constructs also in accordance with the laws of beauty.[7]

Man realizes himself as a man only by realizing nature, by transforming it to his measure, and by becoming a *creator* of culture, of civilization.

Man, then, has rights—over his activity as a conscious producer, over his "expenditure of labor," and over the objects he produces. In the capitalistic system, however, man undergoes a double alienation, a dual frustration, from the fact that he sells to the capitalist his "labor power," which is the source of all human good. The product of his labor is snatched from the producer, in the form of surplus value, to increase the capital. "So much does the performance of work appear as vitiation that the worker is vitiated to the point of starvation."[8] The alienation is not only in the product; it is in production itself which, by its human character, should be *free* activity. In the capitalist system, production is imposed on the producer from the outside. "It is forced labor." It is not the satisfaction of an inner need for creation, "but a means to satisfy needs external" to man. "[It is] the personal physical and mental energy of the worker, his personal life (for what is life but activity?) as an activity which is directed against himself, independent of him and not belonging to him. This is the *self-alienation* as against the alienation of the thing."[9]

Alienated from himself, the salaried producer becomes a stranger to other men behind a screen of objective products. Passively, he is dominated by his products; actively, by his employer, to whom the products belong. Man has become a wolf to man. But the alienation in turn affects the employer, who betrays his human nature. He becomes more and more a parasite, leaving to the technician the role of thinker and inspirer that he himself should play. Thus he destroys the natural harmony of persons and things.

How can one prevent this mutual alienation and, *mutatis mutandis,* regain the natural equilibrium of a patriarchal economy? Here we refer especially to Engels, who is often clearer than Marx though less profound. Before the establishment of capitalism, the productive forces—that is to say, the instruments of production—were weak. They belonged either to the individual or to the family in the framework of family cooperation. Little by little, the factory replaced the individual tools. The work, once individual or cooperative, becomes collective, while the productive forces and the products remain individual and private property is maintained.

This is the imbalance that breaks natural laws and alienates at once both worker and employer. The alienation of the bourgeois lulls him to sleep instead of waking him, but the proletariat, on the contrary, more seriously alienated, is conscious of its physical and moral suffering. Whence class antagonism, which the accumulation of capital and periodic depressions exacerbate, and

which calls for revolutionary solution. Inevitably, the proletariat will one day seize political power and establish its "dictatorship."

"In reality," Marx writes, "it is up to the practical materialist
to revolutionize the existing world, to attack in a practical manner, and to change conditions." It is a matter of restoring to the
productive forces and the products themselves their natural
appropriation, which, under a system of collective labor, can
only be collective. Thus the natural balance will be restored.
Man will stop being dominated by his products and will dominate them. He will institute a planned, rational organization of
production. Only thus will he act on nature instead of being
acted on by nature. Then the totality of goods produced by men
according to each man's capacity will go to the totality of men
according to each man's needs. And man will find his place and
his role in the universe. The reign of *freedom* will then succeed
that of *necessity*.

We have been able to present merely an outline of Marxian
thought. This is difficult to condense into a few pages, for it is
much richer and contains many more nuances than "Marxists"
usually claim. Sometimes it may even seem contradictory. Let us
now examine it with a critical eye.

We may wonder, first of all, whether the socialism and economics of Marx is really "scientific." Yes and no. *No,* if one
means by scientific the exact knowledge and formulation of economic facts in laws that permit one to foresee and to organize
a balanced economy. *Yes,* if science is defined as comprehension
of the real, if it consists of deciphering the complexities basic to
economic facts, and especially man's relations to these facts, and
if its aim is to reveal "the economic law of motion in modern
society."

So we must not seek in Marx, not even in *Capital,* an exposé
of economic laws. Considering them more or less as contingent
"appearances," Marx was not interested in them. Moreover, he
went so far as to predict changes that have not occurred.

In *Conflit du Siècle,* Fritz Sternberg has analyzed almost all the
changes in economic, social, and political reality that have taken
place since the publication of *Capital.* (They have been listed by

other writers.) The changes are important, but in our resumé
of Marx's theories, we skipped over most of them; we shall now
mention only a few, while noting the recent studies made in
France by the Autonomous Socialist Party:

1. The "class struggle" is much more complex than Marx
thought. In fact, the working class is not a simple reality. Moreover, it is diminishing, while the several categories of salaried
workers with dissimilar interests are increasing.

2. The peasants, whom Marx considered more or less im-
pervious to revolutionary ferment and dedicated "to the stupidity
of rural life," have, in underdeveloped countries, belied his
judgment.

3. The theory of capitalist concentration has not been borne
out by the facts. On the contrary, the number of small and
medium-sized businesses continues to grow in Western European
countries.

4. Though periodic economic crises have not ceased, they are
becoming rarer, and we cannot reasonably foresee a general
cataclysm ending the capitalist system, which is adjusting to
economic and social evolution.

5. "Socialism" has not triumphed in the industrial nations of
Western Europe as Marx predicted it would, but in the underdeveloped nations of Eastern Europe and Asia.

By excessive simplification of the "class struggle" theory—a
more precise translation of *Klassenkampf* would be "class war"[10]
—Marx overestimated the role of the determinism of things and
underestimated man's freedom and the organizing power of the
capitalist state. Thanks to trade-union activity and a more enlightened middle class, the capitalist state has been able, by a
policy of intervention and rational organization, progressively
to reduce the surplus-value. This surplus-value, reduced by more
equitable taxation, has permitted the productive investments of
the postwar era and the institution of social security. Marx welcomed social legislation; in his opinion, it would lead to increased
unemployment, bitter class antagonism and, finally, to the revolution. However, social reforms have produced quite the opposite
effects.

We may also observe in passing that Marx did not pay enough

attention to the role of cooperatives as preached by the utopian socialists. We know from the Scandinavian socialist democracies that these have proved their worth. In Western labor unions, a will to reform has replaced a will to revolt. In the Communist countries, the "dictatorship of the proletariat," contrary to the teachings of Marx, has made the state an omnipotent, soulless monster, stifling the natural freedoms of the human being, and drying up the sources of art, without which life is not worth living.

One final word on this point. In Marx's day, colonialism was just beginning. He could not foresee its universal development during the second half of the nineteenth century. He spoke, of course, of "the modern theory of colonization,"[11] but merely in the etymological sense of the word. He had in mind only the European colonization of the United States. Furthermore, his macro-economic theory and almost blind confidence in prole- tarian generosity and conscience prevented him from anticipating the opposition that would develop between colonizers from the dominant countries and proletarians in the dominated territories. It is a now commonplace fact that the European masses' standard of living has been able to rise only at the expense of the standard of living of the masses in Asia and Africa. The economy of Euro- pean nations consists fundamentally in selling manufactured products to underdeveloped countries at high prices and buying raw materials from them at the lowest possible cost. I am not talking about the United States of America. The problem is different with France, but if the prices paid for raw materials in African countries are subsidized, it is no less true that French prices are generally the highest in Europe. One compensates for the other. In a word, the European proletariat has profited from the colonial system; therefore, it has never really—I mean, effec- tively—opposed it.

There we have a series of facts we must think about, we men from underdeveloped countries, men inspired by socialism. We must not consider Marx as an economist like Keynes, but as a sociologist, a philosopher. This would have astonished the founder of "scientific socialism," since he refrained from "phi- losophizing." Yet his thought remains that of a philosopher.

Beyond the economic "appearances," it plunges into the human reality that causes them. For the *factual* view of things, Marx substitutes a profound insight into human needs. His is a new humanism, new because it is *incarnate*.

Humanism, the *philosophy of humanism,* rather than economics, is the basic character and positive contribution of Marxian thought. As we said earlier, Marx does not formulate laws from economic facts; he defines "the economic law of motion of modern society," which is a social "tendency" rather than a law. In his analysis, he advances by *postulates* and theories that explain the facts.

For a better understanding of the philosophy of humanism, we should like to return to the Marxian concept of labor. Here we should add to the extracts from "Alienated Labour" a passage from *Capital,* one of the most beautiful and profound that Marx ever wrote. If labor defines man, primitive man is still only *Homo faber,* scarcely distinguishable from the animal. His labor is an assimilation of nature, a transformation of nature to satisfy his vital needs, just as is animal activity. To the extent that he acts on nature and humanizes it, man acts "on his own nature" and humanizes it at the same time. *Homo faber* becomes *Homo sapiens;* he introduces "consciousness and liberty" as well as artistic feeling into his labor. In so doing, he distinguishes himself from the animal:

> But what from the very first distinguishes the most incompetent architect from the best of bees, is that the architect has built a cell in his head before he constructs it in wax. The labor process ends in the creation of something which, when the process began, already existed in an ideal form. What happens is, not merely that the worker brings about a change of form in natural objects; at the same time, in the nature that exists apart from himself, he realizes his own purpose, the purpose which gives the law to his activities, the purpose to which he has to subordinate his own will. Nor is this subordination a momentary act. Apart from the exertion of his bodily organs, his purposive will, manifesting itself as attention, must be operative throughout the whole duration of the labor.[12]

Thus, if labor defines man, a certain kind of labor makes him more than a man. Man realizes his full potential to the extent that there is division and socialization of labor. From patriarchal cooperation to the factory, man grows gradually in consciousness and in freedom. From master of a tool, he becomes master of the world. But at the same time, he is separated from the world and from himself: grandeur and wretchedness of man in and because of labor. Marx's originality is that starting from purely materialistic postulates, he arrives at a vision of man that yields, neither in truth nor in depth, to that of the greatest philosophers. It recalls the vision of Pascal. This is Marx's positive contribution: an incarnate conception of man based on the material and social determinations of man.

This conception goes further than is generally recognized. In this connection we refer you to an article by Lucien Goldmann, "La Réification."[13] Goldmann tells us that he borrowed the term from Georg Lukacs. Reification appears in the Marxian analysis of value. In capitalist society, mercantile relations gradually replace human relations; consciousness tends in its forms of thought and feeling to empty itself from the inside. Its manifestations—religion, ethics, art, and literature—lose their real, autonomous character as they are invaded by the "ghostly realities" of the economy. *Homo sapiens* becomes *Homo oeconomicus* and regresses to the status of the animal:

> The mercantile economy, and especially capitalist economy, tends, in the producer's consciousness, to replace use-value with exchange-value, and concrete, significant human relations with abstract universal relations between sellers and buyers; thus it tends to substitute the *quantitative* for the *qualitative* throughout human life [Italics mine].[14]

Although Goldmann's thought is shaded, we cannot fully accept his statement that, "In classic capitalist society, only the proletariat is in a situation that allows it to refuse reification and to *restore its true human character to all the spiritual problems* [Again my italics]."[15] As Marx has shown us, the proletarian is in fact victim of the greatest alienation. That is why he avoids labor and takes refuge in the satisfaction of animal needs. His sole superiority over the bourgeois is that he feels his estrangement. If, historically, he refused this alienation, it was

always because of the initiative of less alienated bourgeois intellectuals, who showed him the road to liberation. It is true
that every worker who reflects about problems is already an
intellectual. So it is with colonized people, who are the victims
of a multiple alienation. The intellectuals—often European intellectuals—have awakened them and made them discover their
spiritual, human riches. In truth, and this follows from Marxian
analysis, all Western civilization, all machine-civilization, all fac-
tory-civilization, is reified. We shall see what role the colonized
peoples must play in the struggle for *dereification*.

Along with its positive, revolutionary contributions, however,
Marx's humanism presents a negative aspect. Its weakness is that
it proceeds from a one-sided conception of man and universe, or
perhaps, more exactly, from an equivocal conception. Marx's ambition—and his paradox—has always been to express, throughout his entire work, the dignity of man and his spiritual needs
without ever resorting to metaphysics or ethics or religion, not
even philosophy. He is a philosopher in spite of himself. Moreover, one needs only to re-read Marx carefully to perceive that
his vocabulary, in his numerous lyrical passages, is one of indig-
nation because it is based on an ethic.

In the name of whom or of what, after all, does Marx dare to
affirm the dignity of man and man's right to appropriate all the
products of his labor? In the name of whom, or of what, does
he condemn night labor, child labor, and the African slave trade,
unless it be in the name of a certain quality or a transcendent
something beyond man? Science notes facts and their relations;
it explains, it does not demand. It cannot pass from a factual to
a value judgment. We do not underestimate the strength of the
arguments advanced by Lucien Goldmann in his article "Propos
dialectiques" (subtitled "Y a-t-il une sociologie marxiste?"). Leaning on Max Adler and Georg Lukacs, Goldmann shows that
Marxism is a *sociology*, at once historical knowledge and action,
theory and *praxis*, science and ethics:

> The dialectical position of Lukacs is specifically characterized by the
> refusal to subordinate the means to the end, the end to the means,
> the group to the individual, or the individual to the group, etc. End,
> means, group, individual, party, masses, etc., being in dialectical

thinking elements constituting a dynamic totality, within which it is a question of combating, in each concrete situation, the ever-present danger of the primacy of one or another of these with relationship to the others and to the ensemble.[16]

We agree with Goldmann that Lukacs' position restores the "true inner coherence" to Marx's work. We do not feel that it eliminates "the so-called dualities."

At this point, we must apply to Marx the Marxian method, the historical method. His life and works reveal him to be primarily a philosopher, a pupil of Hegel and Feuerbach; later, in Paris, he studied "economics, the history of the revolution, and socialism. The great thinker Saint-Simon exerted the most considerable influence on him."[17] From the French idealistic sociologists, later termed "Utopian," Marx inherited his concern for ethics. He assimilated, in the etymological sense of the word, German philosophy and French ethics, while transforming them so that they appear only as fine threads in his writing, especially in *Capital*.

As he advanced in his career, Marx gradually placed more and more stress on materialism, means and *praxis,* while the philosophical thought and ethical concerns of his earlier works were toned down. But, although de-emphasized and hidden, they did not disappear entirely. At the risk of becoming repetitious, we may say that they subtend Marx's writings. One can detect in Marx more than a philosophy and an ethic—a metaphysics, a *Weltanschauung,* but brought back from God to man, from the transcendent to the *immanent.* Father Bigo is right to speak of the "ambivalence of Marx." And, in a review of *Capital,* published in the Stuttgart *Observer* on December 27, 1867, Engels put it even more clearly: "Insofar as the book itself is concerned, we must carefully distinguish between the solid, positive presentations and the suggestive conclusions that the author draws from them." Later on, he explained:

It is quite different with the author's subjective conclusions, the manner in which he imagines and presents to others the ultimate result of the present movement of social evolution. This has nothing to do with what we call the positive part of the book. Moreover, if space permitted us to discuss the point, we could perhaps indicate that those *subjective* whims are refuted by his own objective expositions [Engels' italics].

This comment by Marx's most faithful collaborator—indeed, co-author—is not negligible. We need say no more about it. In Marx's work there is a positive contribution and a subjective tendency that contradicts it and reaches debatable conclusions. We need not reject the same conclusions that Engels rejects. Marx's atheism is, in our opinion, the fruit of this subjective tendency.

And yet atheism is deep in Marx; it impregnates his entire work, above all the *Philosophical Writings*. It is basic to him. For Marx, the most complete alienation of man stems from religion, because religion separates man from nature, from society, and from himself in order to enclose him in an abstract world where he cannot realize his potential. In Marx's view, the religious act is the most absolute act of *dehumanization*. To support this contention, we could quote numerous passages; I shall cite only the famous sentence "Religion is the opium of the masses." Nevertheless, appearances to the contrary, atheism is not necessary to the "positive part" of Marx's work. In some of his writings, he even goes so far as to refuse its "mediation."

Historically, Marx's atheism can be explained both by his family environment and by reasons of *praxis*. His father was a Jew who had been compelled to embrace Christianity. Thus young Marx never knew anything but the external practices of religion; he never lived it. Another historical fact is that the triumph of capitalism in Christian countries of the West was accompanied by serious religious deviations. Marx's atheism can be considered as a *reaction of Christian origin against the historical deviations of Christianity,* which violated the essence of religion all the less because the idea of alienation was of religious origin. We find its equivalent in Islam. Later, we shall see a churchman use a similar dialectical approach to materialistic atheism. At this point, we must consider the method employed by the founder of "scientific socialism." This will shed more light on the problem, for method is by all odds Marx's most fruitful contribution.

Socialism Is a Method

You are perhaps astonished that we are proceeding backward, ending where we should have begun: with the problem of method. We have tried to advance by examining Marxian thought thoroughly, by revealing its most secret corners little by little.

Before analyzing Marx's method, we shall try to explain his theory of knowledge, his gnosiology. In a footnote to his articles on "Questions de méthode," Sartre asserts:

> The theory of knowledge is the weak point of Marxism. When Marx writes, "the materialist conception of the world simply means the conception of nature as it is, without any foreign adjunct," he acts as an *objective gaze* and claims to view nature as it is absolutely.[18]

This is true in a certain sense. Marx seems here to claim that man can know the thing "in itself." His definition is one of those tendentious views Engels talks about. Nevertheless, to gain a more correct appreciation of Marxian gnosiology, one must consider a whole set of texts, as Henri Lefebvre does,[19] though Marx dwelt little on the theory of knowledge: *Contributions to the Critique of Political Economics, German Ideology, Eleven Theses on Feuerbach, Capital* (especially the Preface to the second edition).

"The method of inquiry," Marx writes in the last of these, "has to appropriate the *material* in detail, to analyse its different forms of development, to trace out their inner connections."[20] I have italicized the word *material*. This concept of materiality, of matter, is at the heart of Marx's theory of knowledge. Marx does not define it precisely; he merely cites examples: language and, in general, any fact that is "empirically demonstrable." But Lenin says, "The sole 'property' of matter—with the recognition of which materialism is vitally connected—is the property of *being objective reality,* of existing outside of our cognition."[21] In other words, materialism, like idealism, is a postulate, a philosophic interpretation of the world. So much for the concept. As for the concrete qualities of matter, they are discovered and defined by sciences as they develop. For Marx, who is less radical

than Lenin, to know—to seize the truth—is to "appropriate matter in detail." This goes beyond the old materialism, which treats
matter as a "thing in itself," an absolute object outside the
consciousness.

Truth is reality; it comes from confronting subject and object,
from perceiving the object by conscious activity; subject and
object are but the two aspects of a single reality:

> The question whether objective truth is an attribute of human
> thought—is not a theoretical but a practical question. Man must
> prove the truth, i.e. the reality and power, the "this-sidedness" of his
> thinking in practice. The dispute over the reality or non-reality of
> thinking that is isolated from practice is a purely scholastic question.[22]

The basic role that practice plays in knowledge distinguishes
Marx's postulate from Hegel's, and materialism from idealism.
Marx does not deny the role of the mind, he even makes it a
reality, a "matter"—so there is nothing coarse about the term—
but it is matter based on another matter that is even more real:
the empirical fact.

> To Hegel, the life-process of the human brain, *i.e.*, the process of
> thinking, which, under the name of "the Idea," he even transforms
> into an independent subject, is the demiurgos of the real world, and
> the real world is only the external, phenomenal form of "the Idea."
> With me, on the contrary, the ideal is nothing else than the material
> world reflected by the human mind, and translated into forms of
> thought.[23]

But matter that is the object of thought is not matter that
is the object of the so-called exact sciences. It is the human,
social matter of a given century—the nineteenth, and of a given
territory—Western Europe. It is complex, made of reciprocal
reactions of infrastructure and superstructure, economic and cultural facts, things and men. It is composed of contradictions and
is perpetually changing. It is matter animated by dialectical
movement. For dialectics, before it is a method, is the very
movement of "material" realities. The method was, so to speak,
in the movement of things; it was simply a question of disen-
tangling it from practice.

What, then, is dialectics? It is nothing new. To discover its origin, one must go back to the Greeks, to Heraclitus, who first affirmed the mutability and instability of things, their perpetual *becoming*. Hegel, from whom Marx borrowed dialectics, merely reflected on the subject and formulated it.

Today, we define dialectics by opposing it to logic. Classical logic rests on three principles: identity (A is A); noncontradiction (A is not non-A); and exclusion (A cannot be A and not be A at the same time). Hegel, with Marx following in his footsteps, opposes these principles and proposes in their stead the principles of dialectics, which are: contradiction, reciprocal action, and change. For Hegel, the dialectical process is composed of three steps: affirmation, negation, and conciliation. For Marx, it consists of "position, opposition, composition. . . . We have thesis, antithesis, and synthesis . . . [or] affirmation, negation, and negation of the negation."[24] But that is only the beginning. The synthesis or "new idea" is developed "in two contradictory thoughts that blend in turn into a new synthesis" or "group of thoughts." This group, continuing the process and developing into two groups of contradictory thoughts, ends in a "series of thoughts." The entire series of ideas forms the "system" or body of the doctrine.

In classical philosophy, which used logic, things and their concepts are objective realities placed one beside the other without any link or communication, fixed once and for all, immutable essences. They oppose each other in irreducible antitheses. Modern philosophy is quite different, for dialectics is its favorite instrument:

As long as we regard things as at rest and lifeless, each by itself, side by side and one after the other, we certainly do not run across any contradictions whatsoever in them. We find there certain qualities which are in part common, in part differing, even mutually contradictory, but in this case are qualities of different objects and therefore contain in themselves no contradiction. So far as this sphere of observation extends, to that extent we are able to get along with the ordinary metaphysical mode of reasoning. But it is quite different as soon as we observe things in their movement, in their change, in their life, in their reciprocal influence on one another. Here we fall at once into contradictions.[25]

In fact, as Heraclitus noted more than 2,000 years ago, things, like living beings, are in constant change. Within themselves, they contain their own negation (not to mention the reciprocal action of one on the other), inner contradictions that, in developing their natural movement, will lead to the destruction of these things or, more exactly, to their transformation into new syntheses or symbioses, into new realities. "The mystification which dialectic suffers in Hegel's hands by no means prevents him from being the first to present its general form of working in a comprehensive and conscious manner. With him, it is standing on its head. It must be turned right side up again, if you would discover the rational kernel within the mystical shell."[26] And so, Marx and Engels, under the influence of Feuerbach, have substituted *dialectical materialism* for the dialectical idealism of Hegel. Applied to history and to the study of the evolution of human societies, dialectical materialism is also called historical materialism.

We shall refuse to believe—African politicians have often succumbed to the temptation—that "dialectics" solves all problems and dispenses with the need for reflection. Even less shall we believe that the word can justify our cowardice, betrayals, and thoroughly reprehensible electoral tactics. It is rather a conscious and honest attempt to analyze all the data of reality in their specific aspects, reciprocal reactions, and modifications. It neglects no method of investigation, least of all the old logic. For the latter, with its definitions of concepts, its deductions and inductions—not to mention intuition—remains the solid basis for all coherent reasoning.

Dialectics also includes the most effective philosophical and scientific methods of today: existentialism, phenomenology, psychoanalysis. As Sartre says in "Questions de méthode," Marxian thought is merely a framework; we must fill this frame by studying concrete men in concrete situations and with efficient methods. All social reality, particularly cultural reality, cannot be explained simply by the "class struggle." And so we are already engaged in the criticism of "dialectical materialism."

It is difficult to deny the revolution caused by dialectics in philosophy and in the social and exact sciences. Much of the progress accomplished by these sciences since the start of the century must be attributed to it. But to claim with J. B. S. Haldane,[27] that we are indebted to Marx for the latest scientific discoveries would be to exaggerate. Nevertheless, Marx has contributed decisively to the theory of knowledge. Today, truth is no longer considered an absolute that is despotically imposed on our minds. . . .

We are less concerned with criticizing Marx's dialectics than his materialism, even if the latter be dialectical. Let us recall a sentence quoted by Sartre: "The materialistic conception of the world simply means the conception of nature as it is, without any foreign addition." Incontestably, Marx reverts here to the old concept of mechanistic materialism and seems to deny the active role of the subject in knowledge. He becomes a positivist. Once again, there is an "ambivalence" in his thought, a tendency, as he gets farther away from his philosophical writings, to harden his materialistic position, to sacrifice theory to practice.

This tendency appears most of all in his economic and political works: *The Communist Manifesto, Address to the Central Committee of the Communist League, Capital,* and *Critique of the Gotha Programme.* To be sure, one can show that the sentence attacked by Sartre is an isolated instance, that Marx's ultimate aim is to suppress the opposition between idealism and materialism by transcending it. To support this, one can cite one meaningful sentence: "We see here how consistent naturalism or humanism is distinguished from both idealism and materialism, and at the same time constitutes their unifying truth."[28]

Nevertheless, for practical reasons, for the purpose of "changing" the world, Marx becomes increasingly reluctant to "interpret" it. More and more, he turned against the philosophy of his earlier writings and his dialectical method itself in favor of a rigid determinism. By the same token, he opted for a different philosophy, a different metaphysics, a religion. For what is religion if not the link that unites man to the world, an active and impassioned explanation of the universe? Certain atheistic Marxists have recognized this and have observed that Marx borrowed indirectly from the theologians of the Middle Ages and the Church Fathers, not only a certain vocabulary but the idea of alienation and of social justice. Whence the prophecies of the economic and political works, prophecies that events have belied because they are veritable poems of fatality. Subsequently, wave mechanics, quantum theory, and relativity have shaken classical determinism. We are no longer able to accept Marx's vision of the future.

Under these circumstances, it is not surprising that Teilhard de Chardin studied this problem and took issue with Marx. Make no mistake about it: Far from scorning Marx, he considered him one of the rare thinkers worthy of serious attention for having "delved to the bottom of things." Teilhard had the advantage of being a scientist—geologist, pre-historian, anthropologist—as well as philosopher. Four comments are essential at the outset:[29] Teilhard had a phobia against literary people—jurists, sociologists, and other "humanists."[30] It is as a naturalist, as a scientist, that he debated with Marx. For him, the social fact "is really part of the general evolution of matter and life." It was therefore necessary to broaden the base of Marx's starting point (sociology), and include all the natural sciences: physics, chemistry, geology, and biology. For man is primarily a "cosmic phenomenon."[31] Like Marx, Teilhard begins with matter, but in his case its concrete characteristics are more strictly defined, thanks to the recent discoveries of the physicists. He often uses the dialectical method.

Teilhard begins with the concept of energy, the fundamental concept of physics. In *The Phenomenon of Man*,[32] he distinguishes between tangential energy—material energy that can be measured by physicists—and radial, or psychic, energy. In *Les Singularités de l'espèce humaine,* he argues against deterministic materialism by a particularly daring dialectical twist:

> But why, completely reversing the perspective, should we not decide on the contrary that, of the two things considered, it is the radial that is primitive and consistent, the tangential being only a subproduct? . . . If this point of view were accepted, the structure of physical laws would remain absolutely intact and valid in the pre-life, where the radial, for our eyes, still does not exist.[33]

It is a question of subordinating physical energy to psychic energy, of considering the spirit, which has gradually freed itself from matter, as the basic reality. . . .

Thus, starting from concrete facts, on a material basis, but broader and more profound than that of Marx, Teilhard emerges above and ahead on the spiritual level. "As I like to say," he concluded in a letter of May–June 1952, "the synthesis of the Christian 'God' on high and the Marxist 'God' of the future is the only God we can henceforth adore in spirit and in truth." As you know, the Christian God is also the Moslem God.

This, to be sure, is a postulate, but one with formidable revolutionary content. It can revolutionize philosophy and the sciences. For those who, like most of us, are believers, it introduces not only the spirit but freedom at the heart of matter—without abandoning the dialectical method. While allowing us to keep the positive contributions of socialism, it justifies our faith. Just as Christians have attempted a constructive critique of socialism, Moslems have now started a similar study of European (including Marxist) contributions. We shall name only Sheik Abdou, Al Afghani, and Mohamed Iqbal. Their objective is to open Islam to the contemporary world without decreasing its spiritual zeal. All these thinkers, whether Christian or Moslem, show us the road to follow.

For an African Type of Socialism

Let us recapitulate Marx's positive contributions. They are: the philosophy of humanism, economic theory, dialectical method. To these we may add trade unionism, planning, and also federalism and cooperation, which come to us from the French idealistic socialists—Saint-Simon, Proudhon, and Fourier, to name only the outstanding ones.

Thus, we are not *Communists*. Does this mean that we shall practice anti-Communism? Certainly not. Anti-Communism, the "witch hunt," can have but one result: increased tension between East and West and a continuation of the Cold War with the obvious risk of unleashing a third global conflict from which humanity would not recover. We are not Communists for a theoretical reason: Lenin's definition of matter proceeds from a one-sided concept, from a purely materialistic and deterministic postulate. At the beginning of *Anarchism or Socialism,* Stalin goes even further: "Marxism is not only a theory of socialism, it is a definitive view of the world, a philosophical system."

We are not Communists for a practical reason: The anxiety for human dignity and the need for freedom—man's freedoms and freedoms of collectivities—that animate Marx's thought and provide its revolutionary ferment, this anxiety and this need are unknown to Communism whose major deviation is Stalinism. The "dictatorship of the proletariat," which was to be only temporary, becomes the dictatorship of the Party and State in self-perpetuation. "The Soviet Union," said a Senegalese on his return from Moscow, "has succeeded in building socialism, but at the sacrifice of religion, of the soul."

The paradox in the building of socialism in Communist countries, or at least in the Soviet Union, is that it increasingly resembles capitalistic growth in the United States, the American way of life, with high salaries, refrigerators, washing machines, and television sets, but with less art and less freedom of thought. Nevertheless, we shall not be won over to a regime of liberal capitalism and free enterprise. We cannot close our eyes to segregation, although the Federal Government combats it, nor can we accept material success as a way of life.

We stand for a middle course, for a *democratic socialism*, which goes so far as to integrate spiritual values, a socialism which ties in with the old ethical current of the French socialists. Historically and culturally we belong to this current. Besides, the French socialists—from Saint-Simon to the Léon Blum of *For All Mankind**—are not so utopian as they are reputed to be. Insofar as they are idealistic, they fulfill the requirements of the Negro-African soul, the requirements of men of all races and all countries. *Not by Bread Alone*—this is the title of a novel by Dudintsev, a Soviet writer, and the Russians read this book avidly. Khrushchev was not mistaken: De-Stalinization was imposed by the people, by the thirst for freedom, by the hunger for "spiritual nourishment."

---

* Léon Blum (1872–1950), French socialist leader. *A l'échelle humaine* (Paris: Gallimard, 1945) was written in 1941, while the author was in prison. An English translation, by William Pickles, was published in London (Gollancz, 1946). [TRANS.]

Concluding his report on the East German Republic (Communist Germany), Michel Bosquet wrote: "When I ask [the head of a labor union] what the workers demand, he replies: 'Today they want TV set and motorcycles. When they get them, they will demand a shorter work week. And then? . . . I can only answer for myself. What I should like, what I miss, is more good literature.' "[34] This fact is not unrelated to a phenomenon observed in America: the appeal of the contemplative life as a reaction against the surrounding machinism. Among American Catholics, the proportion of priests to laity is one of the highest in the world.

This thirst for freedom, this hunger for spiritual nourishment, strengthened by the moral tradition of French socialism, explains why numerous French Marxists in recent years have shunned Stalinism and even Communism: Henri Lefebvre, Pierre Fougeyrollas, and Edgar Morin, among others, have recently stated their reasons in sorrowful but lucid volumes.[35] The major reason, common to them all, is that the Party has come to submerge the individual under the collectivity, the person under the class, to hide reality behind the screen of ideology. If we reflect on these various cases, we shall discover that, with the exception, perhaps, of Lefebvre, they "call into question" not only Marxism but Marx himself. For if the individual is forgotten, it is because Marx did not pay sufficient attention to the "natural determination," namely, the *Nation,* which is not effaced by class.

Marx underestimated the political and national idealism that, born in France upon the ruins of provincial fatherland, won over the world in the Revolution of 1789. "Justice," Marx writes, "humanity, liberty, equality, fraternity, independence . . . these relatively moral categories that sound so nice but in historical and political questions prove absolutely nothing."[36] I repeat: *independence.* If the creator of scientific socialism returned to this earth, he would perceive with amazement that these "chimeras," as he called them, and above all the concept of *Nation,* are living realities in the twentieth century.

What is left of the Revolution of 1789? A political doctrine and technique, accepted nowadays even by the devout. The "worship of the Goddess Reason" was but a momentary flame. Similarly, Marxism will undergo a sifting process. Of it there will surely remain an economic doctrine and technique, inasmuch as they do not contradict the teachings of Christianity and Islam (far from it). But a third revolution is taking place: a reaction against capitalistic and Communistic materialism that will integrate moral, if not religious values with the political and economic contributions of the two great revolutions. Here the colored peoples, including the Negro African, must play their part and help construct the new planetary civilization. As Aimé Césaire says: "They will not come empty-handed to the rendezvous of give-and-take." Between two world wars, Paul Morand observed: "The Negroes have rendered a great service to America. But for them, one might have thought it impossible to live without a bank account and a bathtub." I am quoting from memory.

Our Need for a Triple Inventory

We must build our own development plan, based on European, socialist contributions and also on the best of Negro-African civilization. Thus we shall merely be putting the lesson of socialism into practice. In his correspondence and even in *Capital,* Marx continued to insist that his theory is not an "open sesame to historico-philosophical theory," and that the conclusions of *Capital,* resulting from a study of the capitalist societies of Western Europe in the mid-nineteenth century, are valid only for that milieu and for that period. They were not even valid for Russia, as his letters to Mikhailovsky and Vera Zasulich indicate.

Before drawing up our development plan, we must therefore study our situation—our present situation—using the dialectical method. On a threefold level, we must prepare: (1) an inventory of our traditional civilization; (2) an inventory of the impact of colonialism and French civilization on our traditional civilization; and (3) an inventory of our economic resources, our needs and potentialities. Our development plan must not be solely economic: It must be social in the broadest sense of the word—political, economic, social, and cultural as well. We insist on this last word.

African politicians have a tendency to neglect culture, to make it an appendage of politics. This is a mistake. These two areas, like the others, are certainly closely connected, each reacting on the other. But if one stops to reflect, culture is at once the basis and the ultimate aim of politics. Remember the labor leader quoted a short while ago, "And then? What I should like, what I miss, is more good literature." He could have added, "Good theater, good painting, good music, etc." Culture is also *basic* in the socialist connotation of the word. It is "the sum of objects, ideas, symbols, beliefs, feelings, values, and social forms that are transmitted from one generation to another in a given society."[37] We can accept this definition, though I usually call that "civilization," reserving the word "culture" for the spirit of civilization. Culture is the very texture of society.

Since the start of the century, ethnologists—not to speak of archaeologists, geographers, historians, musicologists, and linguists—have been making an *inventory of Negro-African civilization.* The Institut Français d'Afrique Noire, the University of Dakar, and Présence Africaine are continuing this research. We should all have in our libraries: *La Philosophie bantoue,* by Reverend Placide Tempels; *Dieu d'eau,* by Marcel Griaule; or simply, *Les Contes de l'Ouest Africain,* by Roland Colin.[38] From these volumes we would learn that Negro-African philosophy, like socialist philosophy, is existentialist and humanistic, but that it integrates spiritual values. We would learn that, for the Negro African, the "vital forces" are the texture of the world and that world is animated by a dialectical movement. We would learn that Negro-African society is collectivist or, more exactly, communal, because it is rather a *communion* of souls than an aggregate of individuals. We would learn that we had already achieved socialism before the coming of the European. We would conclude that our duty is to renew it by helping it to regain its spiritual dimensions.

The sociologists are now making an *inventory of the encounter of civilizations.* Much remains to be done in this field. The work of our African writers and artists is not negligible. They present syntheses, the elements of which must now be analyzed. For we must attain a synthesis of civilizations that retains only the fecund elements of each. The objective is a dynamic *symbiosis*—I mean a cultural blending which, like all blending or grafting, produces a more succulent fruit.

The *inventory of our economic resources* will not be the least important. We must congratulate both the governments of the federated states and the Government of Mali for having thought of it. Senegal and Sudan have, in fact, created *study committees* of competent technicians to examine our various problems and to seek the best solutions: for institutional problems, a committee whose conclusions have helped us to prepare our constitutions; a committee for social problems; another on civil service reform; still another on economic problems.

With respect to the last, it is essential that the plans for economic development be coordinated on the level of the Mali Federation. Senegal has selected Father Lebret's team.* Sudan would be well advised to examine the possibility of doing likewise. The merit of Father Lebret's group is that it is affiliated with the school of economics and humanism and is motivated by an "open socialism" very similar to our own conception.

We have spoken of the Mali Federation. Needless to say, our reflections and proposals are valid for all the states of what used to be called French West Africa, for all the French-speaking Negro-African States. If we apply our reflections and proposals to Mali, it is for the simple reason that the success of the PFA and of *African unity* depends on its success. If Mali succeeds, it will serve as an example and a magnet. Then we will be able to create a single federation which may extend—why not?—from Dakar to Brazzaville.

The development plan must be essentially economic and social. Nevertheless, it must be comprehensive and it must be based on the cultural inventory, so that it will flow into our political future. The economic and social choices will be made in line with our objectives. But it is in line with our point of departure —Negro-African culture—that the socialist contribution must be adapted to our realities.

* Father Louis Joseph Lebret, French author and economist, prepared with his associates Senegal's development plan. He heads a movement in Paris called "Economie et Humanisme." [TRANS.]

For a Strong Federal Democracy

Let us get on to the program proper. We remind you that it is less a question of drawing up a complete and detailed program than of defining the probable course of our development, posing the problems that confront us and indicating orientations. As of now, even before obtaining the results of the triple inventory, we have enough information to indicate guidelines. This may facilitate the task of the researchers.

We shall begin by affirming the *primacy of politics*. Politics, one usually says, is "the art of governing the city." This is an orientation toward a general option. *Man,* depicted in black on the flag of Mali, indicates our general option. This black man, our nearest neighbor, must be advanced in all respects, and must become not only a consumer, but above all a producer, of culture.

The Secretary General of our temporary committee, our comrade Modibo Keita, declared in the projected statutes of the PFA that our first aim is the institution of a *democracy*. Only democracy, the "government by the people and for the people," will allow the Negro African to realize himself. After all, democracy is the traditional form of Negro-African societies.

Our democracy will be *federal* for the reasons indicated in the first part of this report. We do not need to remind you that local diversities with their complementary qualities will enrich the Federation. Inversely, the Federation will preserve those diversities. The decentralized federal structure will be extended in the framework of the federal state to regional and communal collectivities, even into economic and social areas. The Yugoslavian structures, adapted to our realities, will, in this instance serve as a model.

Thus we shall fill the dangerous void now existing between the federal state and the village. Our cadres are bored with their freedom from responsibility. Even when they fill this void by forming militant political groups, they tend to limit their activity to contention over slogans. Regional and communal assemblies, among others, would give them a practical opportunity to exercise their responsibilities. A revolution remains ideological and therefore ineffective so long as it is not translated into concrete

action, which, in transforming the structure, raises the citizens'
standard of living and culture.

The creation of the Negro-African nation by the federal state
must be the primary concern of all PFA militants: The mystique
of the Federation must become their mystique. Let us be careful
to remember: Man does not live by millet and rice alone; he
lives truly and solely on the myths that are his spiritual nourishment. Everything must serve the Federation, be subordinated to
the strengthening and extension of the Federation. The division
of responsibilities will be fixed by federal conferences that unite
the federal government and those of the federated states. It is for
the Federal Assembly to revise the Constitution if the need for
this should arise. The party will see to it that the letter and spirit
of the federal Constitution are respected.

A federal democracy, yes, but a strong democracy. As the Secretary General suggests in his report, we must avoid two dangers:
on the one hand, fascist dictatorship, which one observes in the
antifederalist states; on the other hand, governmental instability,
which was common in France during the Third and Fourth Republics. Both deviations are signs of weakness; in the long run,
they provoke the revolt of the people and the disintegration of
the state.

The Mali Federation, like the federated states, will be a democracy. The electoral law will continue to be impartial, as it should
be, not a law of circumstance cut to the measure of the Government or majority party. Freedom of opinion, speech, press, assembly, and association are guaranteed by the constitutions of
Mali and the federated states—in the antifederalist states also.
But, with us, these freedoms do not exist only on paper; they are
effectively enjoyed and will continue to be so. Above all, the
citizens' right of *free settlement* will be assured, whether or not
they be born in Mali. A democratic policy pays dividends; in
addition, it conforms to our humanitarian ideal. Already public
opinion in Black Africa and France is grateful to us. This is
excellent propaganda for Mali.

The rights of the minority, of the opposition, will therefore be
respected in Mali. They will find their natural and legal limits
in the rights of the majority, the popular will, which is sovereign;

in other words, in the rights of the nation-state. For we are a *quasi-nation,* as François Perroux says.*

Executive stability is guaranteed by our constitutions. We need to assure it in actual practice. It is necessary that governments govern, that they, along with the legislative assemblies, take the initiative of making laws within the framework of the doctrine and program of the majority party. Governments must apply the law firmly, and legislative assemblies must check on the action of the government. It is necessary that the Party—through its congress, executive committee, and board—have the final say in matters of control. Yet, to be effective, the various controls will be general and *a posteriori.* Meddling and harassing controls would not work. Here again, we shall avoid two dangers: granting government action a blank check, and taking away the executive power. The controls must be political, not technical.

Let us return to the rights of the opposition. Its role, certainly, is to criticize. But *criticism* means critical spirit, not the spirit of criticism or systematic carping. In a democracy, criticism must be constructive and serve the general, not factional, interest. At any rate, one cannot grant the opposition more rights than the majority enjoys. The law also applies to the opposition, which is likewise required to observe it. Under the control of the majority party, the governments will take all necessary steps to curb demagogic opposition. They will not tolerate violations of the law, appeals to illegality or to violence, whether the pretexts be religious or racial. This is the democratic sense that we attach to the "dictatorship of the proletariat."

For Rational, Dynamic Planning

If politics is the general art of governing the state, if it is a doctrine, the program, on the other hand, will concern itself chiefly with the economic, the social, and the cultural. The economic part of the Development Plan must envisage social and cultural objectives.

We need not stress the well-known fact that underdeveloped

* François Perroux, professor at the Collège de France, is one of France's most distinguished economists [TRANS.]

countries are entangled in a series of contradictions that must be resolved: contradictions between our sickly undernourishment and our need for productivity; between the low percentage of children enrolled in school and our need for cadres; in general, between our poverty and our retardation in all areas. Illness, ignorance, poverty—such is our lot, such the condition from which we must rescue our people. There can be no doubt that we underdeveloped countries are at the bottom of the scale in sickness and hunger, ignorance and poverty. In addition, our countries are underpopulated. If you are still unconvinced, we refer you to a volume by Father Lebret, *Suicide ou survie de l'Occident*.[39] His statistics are taken from the most authentic sources, the publications of the United Nations. You will also be interested in reading a volume by Georges Balandier, *Le Tiers Monde*.[40]

Our task is enormous. To fulfill it, we must draw up a development plan; even before that, we must arouse our people's faith in their destiny and galvanize all their energy and enthusiasm. It is necessary that the *elites* understand their role and accept their responsibility. Those in privileged positions must be willing to make the heaviest sacrifices.

Our first elite group is the *students*. At twenty, one is enthusiastic and idealistic. That is good. One pounces on books and studies furiously. That too is good. In the intelligence and generosity of our students, we have a precious leaven and admirable potentials. These potentials must be realized, must serve the common good. Our students must understand that to study is to *assimilate;* that the theories they study have been developed in Europe and for Europe; that, in order to serve, these theories must be confronted with Negro-African realities and be applicable to them; that knowledge without experience is but empty smoke. As models, they may take the North African students, who have always trusted the political leaders of their respective countries. The North African students favored autonomy when their leaders were struggling for autonomy; they favored independence when, and only when, their leaders fought for independence. What counts is the *unanimity* of a people, rather than a particular doctrine, however excellent it may be.

Our *elites* also include the labor leaders. They became confused at the time of the referendum. It is time for them to recover; they have already begun to do so. Their role is not to replace the politicians but, over and above professional demands, to help the political leaders to carry out their program. An appreciable number of labor leaders—I refer to the UGTAN —call themselves "Marxists." Kautsky reminds them that the most grievous mistake they could make would be to destroy the unity of the labor movement for theoretical considerations. "A Marxist," he writes, "who would push an argument so far as to cause a split in a militant proletarian organization would not be conforming to the doctrine of Marx, for whom every step forward in a real movement is more important than a dozen programs."[41] And Alioune Cissé* has frankly admitted that the labor unions cannot rightly oppose the majority of the people. This is the lesson to be learned from the referendum.

Let us get to the heart of the problem. At its Constitutive Congress in Cotonou (Dahomey), the UGTAN abandoned the "class struggle" theory. This was a return from the clouds to *terra firma*. There are no classes in our society. But analysis reveals a certain tendency, a "real movement" toward the *formation of classes*. Paradoxically, some labor leaders include in the proletariat the entire union membership, which is composed exclusively of government employees and salaried workers in private employ. But the annual income of an African civil servant is about 360,000 CFA francs; that of a wage earner in the private sector is 180,000 francs; whereas that of a peasant in the former French West Africa is 10,000 francs. The proletarian is not necessarily the one who claims that title.

When the unions, especially those of government employees, demand a raise in salary, the African governments, *in the light of present conditions,* can justifiably object on two counts. The first is that their present wages, when converted into metropolitan francs, are, on any given level, at least equal to those received by metropolitan employees. There is admittedly a disparity if we consider wages paid in private employment. But the

* Alioune Cissé is a Senegalese labor leader, at present Senegal's Ambassador to Guinea. [TRANS.]

most important objection stems from a comparison between the living standards of city dwellers—civil servants, workers, and laborers—and of the peasants who constitute more than 90 per cent of the population. It could not serve the public interest to increase the disproportion between the living standards of the classes now in process of formation.

Our Negro-African situation is not identical to the situation in France, where wage-earners are struggling to snatch a larger share of the national income from a bourgeois state. In Africa, we and you are the state. At least the overwhelming majority of top officials and civil servants are Africans. It is against themselves that the labor unions, particularly the government employees, are struggling. This is an unnatural contradiction.

Does this mean that we should do nothing for the government workers? We are not saying that. What we are saying is that our economic and financial situation is not that of France; we have to forget that comparison. We have already forgotten it. The living standard of our government employees should be higher than that of our peasants, but we cannot do less than to fix a relationship between the living levels of our quasi-classes. As the peasants' standard of living rises, in the same proportion we would raise that of government employees and salaried workers in private employment. However, to raise the peasants' standard of living, it is indispensable that we invest productively in agriculture. This implies an increase in our budgets and, accordingly, a temporary freezing of salaries.

In France, government workers constitute 17 per cent of the adult population and are paid 25 per cent of the budget. In Senegal, they constitute only 1 per cent of the population, but are paid 48 per cent of the budget! These figures require no commentary. We believe that civil servants as well as students will appreciate the dramatic situation facing our governments. To renounce productive investments would place us in a vicious circle and require that we beg France to balance our budgets; this would in fact mean renunciation of all political autonomy. Government workers will understand their role in the building of the nation and will accept the sacrifices asked of them. The peasants are already enthusiastic—one has only to note their confidence in the party and in our governments. The labor unions must do even more. They must integrate themselves into the quasi-nation. The UGTAN, for example, must be converted into a General Union of the Workers of Mali and establish its headquarters here; later it will be free to enter a Confederation of the Workers of Black Africa.

This general enthusiasm must help the federal state to build the nation, but it must first help us to achieve our *Development Plan*. This plan requires the investment of substantial sums that will come from three sources: (1) the budgets of Mali and of the federated states; (2) the Community's Fund for Aid and Co-operation (FAC) along with the European Fund; and (3) private capital. Let us review these three sources.

The Budgets. We shall begin by aiding ourselves, in the hope that heaven and others will then aid us. This is a matter of *dignity* and efficiency. It is not right for us to expect assistance from France without having first balanced our basic budget and begun to invest in our own resources. Beggars are never respected. Moreover, as you know, whoever supplies the money exercises political control over the use of the funds. One cannot hope for political autonomy, much less independence, without practicing economy. That is obvious. Admittedly, for populations like ours that increase at the rate of almost 3 per cent each year, we would have to invest 20 per cent of the national income in order to maintain the living standard at the same level year by year. Since Mali has an income of about 140 billion CFA francs, we would have to invest 28 billion annually. We have nothing like that amount available. In any event, we must begin by investing 20 per cent of our budgets, or 8 billion francs. Then we shall be able to find the rest more readily elsewhere.

The FAC and the European Fund represent the second source of investment. If we begin by making a collective effort, if we also prepare solid proposals, there is every chance we shall obtain satisfaction—provided our representatives on the Executive Council are careful to see that the funds are objectively shared and to remember that the effort of austerity and budgetary severity is incumbent on each state in Black Africa. Our membership in the French Community must create no inferiority complex whatever

in us. Every community presents advantages and disadvantages—
more advantages than disadvantages—rights and responsibilities.
If we were independent, we would nonetheless turn to states more
fortunate than ourselves: to European nations and to the U.S.A.,
probably to both. We would only be changing guardians—you
see the disadvantages; at the worst, we could turn to everybody,
thus bringing the Cold War ever closer to us. This would serve
neither our interests nor peace.

The problem of *private capital* remains. We shall not scorn
private capital; instead, we shall seek it, whether from France or
elsewhere, provided it does not alienate the rights of our quasi-
nation. . . . There is a semblance of contradiction between our
socialistic ideal and the aid we request of capital. Analysis reveals
that the contradiction is only superficial and that it can be resolved if indeed it really exists. We shall point out that "the
accumulation of capital," its formation, is necessary to the development of every modern state. In this respect, there is no difference between a capitalist and a socialist state.

In addition, there can be no question of nationalization in an
underdeveloped nation. Neither Guinea nor Ghana is nationalizing. They are right. This is because one has to have something
to nationalize. To nationalize the meager capital at our disposal,
even if we were already independent, would mean "killing the
goose that lays the golden eggs," preventing other urgently
needed capital from being invested. Economists note that in order
to nationalize, one must have the necessary cadres, which is not
true in our case. Even in these circumstances and in developed
countries, nationalization does not always succeed. One final argument: Since capitalists train and employ African personnel, re-
invest part of their profits, and pay taxes, capital is, for all practical purposes, nationalized.

Does this mean that we shall adopt a policy of *laissez-faire?* No.
The negative aim of the development plan is to prevent a *laissez-
faire* economy. Its positive aim is to organize production rationally. Our plan will include three sectors: a socialized sector—
agriculture; a mixed sector—public utilities and semigovern-
mental societies; and a free sector. The latter—banks, commerce,
industry—will itself be oriented toward the objectives of the Plan

and, to a certain extent, controlled. How? By a long-term moratorium on taxes, accorded either to new investments or to enterprises that enter the framework of the Plan. In return, capital in this sector will be expected to accept social legislation and even to cooperate in building the social infrastructure: schools, dispensaries, housing, cooperatives. At this point I may add that until now the trade unions have neglected the creation of cooperatives of production and consumption. Yet, in the Scandinavian countries, cooperation is socialism's most effective instrument.

The mixed sector will preferably comprise transports and power, within the limits of our possibilities, of course. As for agriculture, we are fortunate that it has traditionally been socialistic, given its communal nature in Negro-African society. Once again, we say *communal* and not *collective,* as some usually say. Our agricultural society was more than collective. It did not comprise an aggregate of individuals but was strongly structured, made up of family cooperatives in the framework of the village mutual. The basis of the latter was religious feeling, which gave its members a single soul, a high ideal of solidarity in which all communed. Our new mutuals and cooperatives, integrating all the peasants, will be similarly structured and *animated* by the same ideal.

And why do we need capital? This is the final question that we must answer. We need it for *productive investments.* Only the development of production along with a more equitable distribution of the national income can make Mali a modern state. This is a *sine qua non* for the transformation of the quasi-nation into a nation.

We are just beginning to realize that the most productive investment is the human investment. By that we do not mean what is now referred to as forced labor. (We feel, incidentally, that some day—the sooner the better—we must employ in useful labor the soldiers excused from military service. In the rural communities, we shall even reach the point of having secondary roads built by the villages themselves.) What we do have in mind here are such questions as the training of cadres, schooling, acculturation, and finally nutrition. The human investment will permit the national

State to train citizens—cultivated men, properly fed, and trained in a trade or profession.

The expression "Africanization of cadres" is frequently used and abused. I shall not say "Malianization of cadres," for ours will not consist solely of persons from Mali. We fear the problem is incorrectly phrased. If our educated elite were sufficiently numerous, the question would not need to be raised. But we lack professors, physicians, engineers, researchers, above all, specialists in finance and economics. It is often difficult for us to recruit them even in France. Consequently, the problem is not political, it is technical, for it is a matter of *training African cadres*. This is not the same thing. Let us be careful not to substitute a political problem for a technical problem. That is a mistake often made by political leaders in underdeveloped countries. For a long time yet we shall need technicians from France. We must attract them, not discourage them by untimely words and gestures.

The University of Dakar offers us an Institute of Higher Administrative Studies and an Institute of Higher Economic and Commercial Studies, not to mention the Institute of Human Sciences. This is our good fortune. We can create other centers of apprenticeship and vocational schools for workers and secondary cadres. And, above all, we have at our disposal the great scientific and technical schools of France, which rank among the best in the world. We shall also mention research institutes, for we need research workers. The development of production, linked with that of productivity, is directly dependent on the development of scientific research. In other words, our students will be oriented in their studies. The role of the school is not to give courses in political philosophy, but rather to provide us with highly qualified technicians. The Federal Scholarship Commission of former French West Africa too often tended to orient all our students toward the University. We shall react by directing them toward courses preparing for the competitive examination for admission to the *Grandes Ecoles.**

This brings up the question of schools. Everyone agrees that

* The *Grandes Ecoles* include such institutions as the Higher Normal School, Polytechnic Institute, School of Public Works, etc. [TRANS.]

elementary instruction should be developed. Then we shall have a broader base from which to choose for our secondary schools, for our universities and *Grandes Ecoles*. It so happens that it would take our total budget to provide schools for our entire school-age population. In developed countries, 20 per cent of the budget is allocated to instruction in the most favorable cases. We can do no better. We hope to compensate for our meager means by raising the *quality* of instruction.

Whoever says quality says Africanization of instruction, and this means *education*. On the elementary level, we shall adapt our textbooks to our social and cultural realities. It is unthinkable that our pupils should henceforth be ignorant of the history, geography, and art of Black Africa. Something has already been done in this direction; the effort must be carried through. It is a mistake to cultivate only our youngsters' reason and overlook their creative imagination. The race for the B.A. degree is sterile in France; it is *homicidal* in Africa. Even more, we must educate those who do and those who do not know how to read, outside of school. We must accomplish this by folk festivals, by political, trade-union, and athletic events, by the theater and motion pictures, but still more by lectures and cultural clubs. We take this opportunity to thank the Federal Minister of Education for his excellent initiative in creating a Service of Arts and Letters. It is a matter of simultaneously *acculturating* French instruction and our traditional values to our situation.

Education, cultural and vocational training, are forms of the human investment, though not the only ones. They require, from the outset, that man be properly fed. What a man eats is more important than how much he eats. Our populations suffer less from undernourishment than from malnutrition. They do not have a sufficient quantity of calories or animal proteins. In this connection, United Nations documents show that the populations of West Africa are the most poorly nourished. These nutritional deficiencies, along with lack of hygiene, are the principal causes of so-called endemic tropical diseases, which are really "mass maladies."

Any plan that neglects the human investment will be doomed to failure. To produce, it is necessary to feed, teach, and train the producers. These facts will govern the distribution of funds, which must be devoted, in part, to the human investment, the development of the social infrastructure: schools, dispensaries, hospitals. Then we must direct our attention to productive investments.

We shall insist on the credits intended for *agriculture,* mutuals, and cooperatives, for the modernization of agricultural methods, cattle-raising, and fishing. Mao Tse-tung understood this and went beyond Marx's instructions on this point. The Russians made the mistake of neglecting the peasants and agriculture. Mao Tse-tung did not repeat this error: He depended on the peasants; his revolution was primarily a peasant revolution. To neglect agriculture for industry is, even in advanced countries, to upset the balance and restrict a rising standard of living, not to mention the danger of arousing the peasantry, which is almost always the largest class. Our countries are fundamentally agricultural. We do not merely risk an imbalance to the disadvantage of agriculture. What we risk is developing industry at the expense of food. The case of Senegal is typical.

On the other hand, there is no developed country without industry. The creation of heavy industry does not concern us at the moment. We have no army to maintain and our aims must be governed by our means, which are limited. Moreover, we lack the prerequisites for heavy industry. We have no coal and no electricity except in the form of potential, which is low. Wisdom dictates that we should develop what we have: processing industries, the raw materials for which are found at home or nearby.

Agriculture, livestock, fishing—in Mali we have the finest cattle and the most plentifully stocked fishing waters in West Africa—can be the basis for our processing industries. These are the poles of development, this is the direction our investments will take. Obviously, this must all be studied carefully and then coordinated by the Mali authorities. Overlapping and duplication, competition and bottlenecks between Senegal and Sudan will be avoided. We shall not forget to investigate our potential in minerals. Only half of Senegal has been prospected; in Sudan, nothing has been done in this respect. Nor shall we forget the development of the *general infrastructure:* harbors, airfields, roads. These are the pathways to development, to civilization.

Conclusion

Let us harvest our thoughts. The ultimate aim of the Party of African Federation is the construction of a *Negro-African Nation* in West Africa, which would correspond to a Central African Nation. For *nation* is the first reality of the twentieth century. These nations will comprise the former French colonies in Black Africa. They will be inspired by the ideal of socialism, but it will be an "open socialism." Within this perspective, they will be grouped in federal states. These states will have as their objective the progress of man, by raising his standard of living and culture. The ways and means will be a strong democracy and a planned economy.

The second reality of the twentieth century is the *interdependence* of races, continents, and nations. François Perroux illustrates this truth in a recent article on Guinea.[42] In it he notes that nominal independence is an advantage but that it is not self-sufficient; that Guinea faces the task of constructing her real independence in terms of the international framework of the economy in which she is placed; that she can neither disregard its structures nor break with her own immediate historical past without danger; that, in view of these realities, a development plan cannot be prepared, much less fulfilled, in the narrow limits of a national territory.

"The main weakness of that kind of independence that is achieved at all costs, of that nationalism that is obsessed by the charms of legal sovereignty," he concludes, "arises from the fact that the modern state is *de-territorialized on the African continent as in all other parts of the world.*" Let us stress the point. Common terms that arouse deep emotional reactions and express aspirations that can be clearly observed—such as sovereignty, independence, autonomy, collective will, the will of the state—can no longer be used interchangeably, despite the frequent tendency to do so. A territorial sovereign state on the pattern of Western institutions is strictly speaking neither the necessary requisite nor, obviously, the sufficient requisite for a set of populations to determine itself, discover or re-discover the values of its own civilization, or increase its productivity and standard of living.

We speak of independence; we shall speak of it again. It would be neither honest nor effective to talk of "immediate independence." General de Gaulle offered this to us on September 28, 1958. We did not take it. Let us have the logic and the courage of our convictions. We thought then, as we continue to think, with François Perroux, that "the real powers by which sovereignty is exercised today are, for all nations, a function of effective alliances and coalitions."[43] We believed then, and we still believe that the Community—presented as a dynamic entity in the Constitution of October 4—is the ideal framework for an effective coalition, an association.

French technicians are in demand throughout the world. Whereas the great nations of Europe and America allot only 1 per cent of their national income to aid underdeveloped countries, France allots 2 per cent. Finally, the French have always spoken up in favor of the emancipation of the colored peoples. It is they who have produced the most important and impressive anticolonialist literature. Those are facts, and one cannot argue successfully against facts. Let us speak therefore of transforming the Community into a *multinational confederation*.

We shall nevertheless be mindful of Guinea and the Arab Maghreb. They were linked with us in the old regime. They are our African neighbors. Their intellectuals were trained in French schools. Under the aegis of the French Community, we must reach economic and even cultural agreements with them, and wait for the Community to evolve to the point where it allows us to forge political ties.

Nor shall we forget our African neighbors who speak English. But let us be frank: They should not ask us to leave the Community while they remain in the Commonwealth. Horizontal inter-African solidarity will gradually be established, by beginning with economic and cultural relations. Vertical solidarity between ourselves and our European metropoles will be modified but not dissolved. We shall obtain peace neither by race war nor nor by continental war.

Man remains our first consideration: He constitutes our *measure*. That is what the man on the flag of Mali represents, with his roots in the soil and his eye turned heavenward. I shall end by paraphrasing Dostoevsky, the Russian. A nation that refuses to keep its rendezvous with history, that does not believe that it bears a unique message—that nation is finished, ready to be placed in a museum. The Negro African is not finished before he even gets started. Let him speak; above all, let him act. Let him bring, like a leaven, his message to the world in order to help build the Civilization of the Universal.

The African
Road to Socialism:
Attempt at
a Definition*

Each of you has found in his folder my Report to the Constitutive Congress of the PFA and an article I wrote in
1948 on Marxism and Humanism. You will also find a
selected bibliography—socialist works and criticisms of those
works—as well as numerous passages that highlight the essential
points of the socialist doctrine, more specifically, of its method.

It is not a question today of rejecting that method; we must
rethink it *in the light of African realities*. Still more precisely, we
must face our *Malian realities* in order to develop a new method
that is more appropriate for understanding our realities and
transforming them effectively. The time for philosophizing has
passed; the time for action has come. We must gird up our loins
and assume all our responsibilities as political militants here and
now. These responsibilities can be summed up in a single sentence: We must transform our quasi-nation into a nation, our
underdeveloped country into a developed country, by raising the
standard of living and culture for all the citizens of our respective
states.

A Prerequisite: Cultural Independence

For fifteen years, since the liberation of France, Africans have
been struggling against *colonialism*. This was natural and legit-

* *Speech delivered at the first Young Seminar of the PFA, May 16–19, 1960.*

67

imate, for colonialism is the political and economic dependence of one people on another. Obviously, the personality of a people cannot flower without freedom to develop, and there can be no freedom without specific liberties. There can be no freedom in the total alienation that results from colonialism; there can be no freedom if one's original being is stifled; there can be no independence in dependence. That is what justified the struggle against colonialism.

Our error was not that we fought with the weapons of colonialism—most African politicians, though not all, unfortunately, are anticolonialist—but with the weapons of Europe. To fight colonialism, we borrowed the weapons of the European proletariat, who told us that their struggle and our own were identical. Similar, perhaps, but not identical, for our situations are not the same, as Jean-Paul Sartre showed in *Orphée noir*.[1] In fact, the European proletarians are held in dependent status as individuals grouped in a class, not as a race or a people. As for us, we have been colonized, to be sure, as underdeveloped, defenseless individuals, but also as *Negroes* or Arab-Berbers—in other words, as people of a different race and different culture. This was the basic argument of the colonizer. We were "primitive" and ugly to boot; it was necessary to expose us to progress, to "the light of civilization." Naturally, progress and civilization could only be European.

This problem of civilization was the crucial point of the debate at the Rome Conference (February, 1960) between the European Society of Culture and the African Society of Culture. The Europeans claimed to be the only ones who had envisaged culture in its universal dimensions. From there it was only a step, which had already been taken years earlier, to maintain that European civilization was identified with the Civilization of the Universal and thus should be adopted as *the* Universal Civilization. We had little difficulty in demonstrating that each "exotic civilization" had also thought in terms of universality, that Europe's only merit in this regard had been to diffuse *her* civilization throughout the world, thanks to her conquest and techniques.

To return to the so-called solidarity between the European proletariat and the colonized peoples, this is a romantic theme popularized in Europe, but it does not stand analysis. In actual fact, European conquest and colonization benefited not only the capitalistic bourgeoisie, but also the European middle classes and proletariat. It permitted the emigration of "poor whites" to the colonized countries, the conquest of exotic markets, easy sources of raw materials. Consequently, it favored the industrial development of Europe and a higher living standard for the European masses. This was true—let us have the courage to recognize it—in both Eastern and Western Europe. The proof is that Soviet Russia did not grant independence to her Asiatic republics, particularly not to the Islamic republics. I refer you to the volume by Monteil, *Les Musulmans soviétiques*.[2]

I have said all this to show that independence of the spirit, *cultural independence*, is the necessary prerequisite of other independences: political, economic, and social. This is why I began the second part of my *Report* with a critique of European socialism. My purpose was to show that this socialism, even the "scientific socialism" of Marx and Engels, cannot be accepted in its present form—as too many African intellectuals do, whether they be students or trade unionists—for three reasons.

The first is that the knowledge of Marx and Engels was conditioned by their era, by the rather limited progress of science and philosophy. Against these two socialist thinkers we can invoke the argument Engels himself used against Hegel: "Although Hegel, was—with Saint-Simon—the most universal intellect of his time, yet he was limited first through the necessarily limited extent of his own knowledge and second, by the limitations in breadth and depth of the knowledge and outlooks of his epoch."[3] Though Marx and, especially, Engels had been able to assimilate the latest discoveries—such as the "kinetic theory of gases" and "white corpuscles"—they could not foresee wave mechanics, quantum theory, or relativity. I developed this argument at some length in my *Report* and need not insist on it here.

Secondly, a new theory of knowledge was born during the first half of this century as a result of those scientific revolutions. Dialectics as a theory—more precisely, as a method of knowledge —is not new. The Greek philosopher Heraclitus used it 2,500 years ago. But Hegel renewed it by systematizing it. The merit of

Marx is that he rationalized it, applying it to concrete facts and setting it on its feet. I refer you to Marx's *Poverty of Philosophy*, though I should rather recommend Engels' *Dialectics of Nature* and the *Anti-Dühring*, which are clearer. Even with Marx and Engels, European dialectics remains abstract, fairly close to logic, for it retained the latter's categories and concepts, inductions and deductions. It is still deterministic, and this is partly why twentieth-century thinkers have developed a new method. You will find it explained in the introduction to Gaëtan Picon's *Panorama des idées contemporaines*.[4]

This new method, once again, is born of the new scientific revolutions: relativity, wave mechanics, quantum theory, para-Euclidian geometry, theories of the discontinuous and undetermined. And also from the new philosophical revolutions: phenomenology, existentialism, Teilhardism. The discontinuous and the undetermined are revealed, after the most minute, most advanced, and most exciting research, to be at the bottom of everything. All disciplines are split today into still more specialized disciplines. Sociology is distinguished from ethnology, interpsychology, and social physics. Better still, "there are several geometries, several possible logics, mentalities, irreductbile psychological structures."[5] In this new view of the world, the *real* itself—the same reality—seems multiple to us, at least with multiple, contradictory faces.

Because the real now appears to the European as "a discontinuous and perhaps undetermined reality," he has abandoned his Western method of objectivity, or rather, *"he has integrated it into a new method."* As Picon observes, until the twentieth century, the European always separated himself from the object in order to know it. He kept it at a distance. I add that he always killed it and fixed it in his analysis to be able to use it in practice. "Always," says Picon, "the Western philosophical tradition required this distance for observation; always it tried to retire from the confused melee where, in existence, glances and objects are blurred, and to substitute contemplation for an embrace."[6] The same is true of scientific tradition. This "visual realism" that Picon talks of was not completely discarded by Marx and Engels, even when they applied dialectics to reality. The new method—scientific, philosophical, artistic—is the opposite of this realism:

> We are witnessing a general revision of the idea of objectivity. Everywhere the searcher is involved in his own research, unveiling it only by veiling it. The light of knowledge is no longer an unchanging glare that is cast upon the object without touching it and without being touched by it: It is the dim fulguration born of an embrace, the flash of a contact, a participation, a communion. Modern philosophy means to be an experience, an actual identification between that which has been experienced and reality. In human science, explanation and comprehension are opposites: To grasp the meaning of a human fact is to grasp it in itself and in oneself.[7]

Thus, to know an object, it no longer suffices to see it, to dissect it, to weigh it, even if one has the most perfect precision instruments. One must also touch it, penetrate it from the inside —so to speak—and finger it. To know a human fact, psychological or social, no longer means to investigate it with the aid of statistics and graphs, but to live it: like the white man who, to understand the situation of Negro Americans, blackened his skin with a chemical product and worked as a Negro shoe-shine boy. This is what phenomenological or existential thought reveals, as it follows the path of Marxism and exceeds it while integrating it. In this school of thought, the real coincides with thought, the content of a statement coincides with the form in which it is expressed, philosophy blends with science, as art merges with existence, with *life*. There is more than coincidence here, there is *identity*. In the act of knowledge, one must probe beneath the crystallizations of appearances and education into the primordial chaos unshaped by reason. As Kierkegaard says in his *Journal,* it is a question of "letting the thoughts appear with the umbilical cord of the initial fervor." Like the marveling child. Thus, knowledge is less a creation than a discovery, less a discovery than a rediscovery. More specifically, knowledge coincides with the *essence* of a thing in its innate and original reality, in its discontinuous and undetermined reality, in its *life*.

The reader of Marx and Engels is sometimes tempted, as was J. B. S. Haldane,[8] to believe that we owe the latest scientific and philosophical discoveries to them. A closer reading must convince us that this is not quite accurate. More than Hegel, no doubt, for whom Thought and absolute Reason create reality, Marx and Engels attain the real itself in its movement, but, though they embrace it, they do not penetrate it. They remain determinists, therefore abstract. For them, "things . . . [in] the connection between them . . . their coming into being and passing away, their motion,"[9] are reflected exactly in man's brain, like "copies." They remain determinists and more or less abstract, like Aristotle, Descartes, Spinoza, and Kant, whom Engels denounces as dialecticians who have not exhausted all the resources of the method but whom he nonetheless hails as dialecticians.[10] In other words, the method of "scientific socialism" still falls short of the contemporary method of knowledge.

On closer scrutiny, this knowledge by confrontation and intuition is Negro-African knowledge. This is our third reason for not accepting the theory of European "scientific socialism" in its present form and without prior examination. From our ancestors, we have inherited our own method of knowledge. Why should we change it when Europeans now tell us it is the very method of the twentieth century—and the most fruitful method?

Let us then consider the Negro African as he faces the object to be known, as he faces the Other: God, man, animal, tree or pebble, natural or social phenomenon. In contrast to the classic European, the Negro African does not draw a line between himself and the object; he does not hold it at a distance, nor does he merely look at it and analyze it. After holding it at a distance, after scanning it without analyzing it, he takes it vibrant in his hands, careful not to kill or fix it. He touches it, feels it, *smells* it. The Negro African is like one of those Third Day Worms,* a pure field of sensations. Subjectively, at the tips of his sensory organs, his insect antennas, he discovered the Other. Immediately he is moved, going centrifugally from subject to object on the waves of the Other. This is more than a simple metaphor; contemporary physics has discovered universal energy under matter: waves and radiations. Thus the Negro African *sympathizes,*†

* An allusion to the Age of Reptiles. [TRANS.]
† In the French text, *sym-pathise*, literally, "feels with." [TRANS.]

abandons his personality to become identified with the Other, dies to be reborn in the Other. He does not assimilate; he is assimilated. He lives a common life with the Other; he lives in a symbiosis. To use Paul Claudel's expression, he "knows* the Other." Subject and object are dialectically face to face in the very act of knowledge. It is a long caress in the night, an embrace of joined bodies, the act of love. "I want you to feel me," says a voter who wants you to know him well. "I think, therefore I am," Descartes writes. The observation has already been made that one always thinks something, and the logician's conjunction "therefore" is unnecessary. The Negro African could say, "I feel, I dance the Other; I am." To dance is to discover and to re-create, especially when it is a dance of love. In any event, it is the best way to know. Just as knowledge is at once discovery and creation—I mean, re-creation and recreation, after the model of God.

Young people have criticized me for reducing Negro-African knowledge to pure emotion, for denying that there is an African "reason" or African techniques. This is the hub of the problem; I should like to explain my thought once again. Obviously, there is a European civilization and a Negro-African civilization. Anyone who has not explained their differences and the reasons for them has explained nothing and has left the problem untouched.

Thus, I explain myself. However paradoxical it may seem, the vital force of the Negro African, his surrender to the object, is animated by reason. Let us understand each other clearly; it is not the *reasoning-eye* of Europe, it is the *reason of the touch,*

---

* Here again the word is separated, *con-naît*, literally, "is born with." [TRANS.]

See Arthur Koestler, *The Lotus and the Robot* (New York: The Macmillan Co., 1961) p. 43:

The traditional Eastern way of looking at things is to deny that there *are* things independently from the act of looking. The objects of consciousness cannot be separated from the conscious subject; observer and observed are a single, indivisible, fluid reality, as they are at the dawn of consciousness in the child, and in the cultures dominated by magic. The external world has no existence in its own right; it is a function of the senses; but that function exists only in so far as it is registered by consciousness, and consequently has no existence in its own right.

better still, the *reasoning-embrace,* the sympathetic reason, more closely related to the Greek *logos* than to the Latin *ratio.* For *logos,* before Aristotle, meant both reason and the word. At any rate, Negro-African speech does not mold the object into rigid categories and concepts without touching it; it polishes things and restores their original color, with their texture, sound, and perfume; it perforates them with its luminous rays to reach the essential surreality in its innate humidity—it would be more accurate to speak of subreality. European reasoning is analytical, discursive by utilization; Negro-African reasoning is intuitive by participation.

Young people in Black Africa are wrong to develop a complex and to believe the latter inferior to the former. "The most beautiful emotion that we can experience," wrote the great scientist Einstein, "is mystic emotion. It is the germ of all art and all true science." To return to Negro-African speech, I refer you to two significant articles. The first, "Ethnologie de la parole," is by Maurice Leenhardt,[11] the second, "Introduction à l'étude de la musique africaine," is by Geneviève Calame-Griaule and Blaise Calame.[12] Leenhardt studies the New Caledonians, who are blacks; he contends that the New Caledonian meaning of the *word* is related to that of Negro Africans; the Calame article confirms this. For him, therefore, the black word, "uttered under the shock of *emotion"* (my italics) surpasses that emotion. Coinciding with the real, it is not only an expression of knowledge, but knowledge itself, ready for action, already action. "The word," he concludes, "is thought, speech, action." Now you will understand why, in my definition of Negro-African knowledge, I rejected abstract analysis on the European pattern, why I preferred to use analogous imagery, the metaphor, to make you *feel* the object of my speech. The metaphor, a symbolic short-cut in its sensitive, sensual qualities, is the method par excellence of Negro-African speech.[13]

Today, it is also, quite often, the style of European speech, as Gaëtan Picon indicates. So, our young people should not repudiate the Negro-African method of knowledge since, once again, it is the latest form of the European method. *Participation* and *communion*—those are Picon's words; they are the very words that ethnologists specializing in the study of Negro-African civilizations have used for decades.

Does this mean, as certain young people would like to interpret my remarks, that the Negro African lacks discursive reason, that he has never used any? I have never said so. In truth, every ethnic group possesses different aspects of reason and all the virtues of man, but each has stressed only one aspect of reason, only certain virtues. No civilization can be built without using discursive reason and without techniques. Negro-African civilization is no exception to this rule: Witness the astonishment of the earliest European navigators disembarking in Africa to discover well-organized states, with government, administration, justice, and army, with techniques (remarkable for that date) for working in wood, ivory, bronze, iron, basketry, weaving, and terra cotta, with medical and agricultural techniques worthy of Europe.

From all that, I will conclude that we must maintain the Negro-African method of knowledge, but integrate into it the methods Europe has used throughout her history—classical logic, Marxian dialectics, and that of the twentieth century. Negro-African reason is traditionally dialectical, transcending the principles of identity, noncontradiction, and the "excluded middle." Let us merely be careful not to be led astray by the narrow determinism of Marxism, by abstraction. Let us hold firmly to the *concrete,* and we shall find, underlying the *concrete,* beyond the *discontinuous* and the *undetermined,* the liberty that legitimates not only our faith but the *African Road to Socialism.*

Toward a West African or Negro-Berber Humanism

As we said at the Constitutive Congress of the PFA, "scientific socialism" made two revolutionary contributions to contemporary thought: dialectics and humanism. Not that it invented either the method or the ethic; but it had the merit of inserting them in reality, of embodying them in man's historical determinations —material and social.

In the preceding pages, I have tried to indicate how we are to surpass dialectical materialism by taking our inspiration both from the European method of today and from the Negro-African method of all time. By a remarkable stroke of luck, these two methods now coincide.

As for Marxian humanism, which we now propose to discuss, I wish first of all to recall its strength and its weakness. Its strength is that, starting from concrete facts, it elaborated the sociological realities which the analysis of European society in the mid-nineteenth century revealed: the priority of the economic factor and the class struggle. Its strength is also that it pointed out and renewed the notion of *alienation*. Its weakness is that it did not carry the economic analysis far enough: It neglected *statistics,* albeit the embryonic statistics then existing. Its weakness lies above all in the fact that, as Marx proceeded in his writing of *Capital,* he increasingly stressed materialism and determinism, *praxis* and means, to the detriment of dialectics and ethics—in a word, to the detriment of man and his freedom. I shall no longer say, as I did in my *Report,* to the detriment of philosophical thought; for, rejecting the spirit of his *Philosophical Works,* Marx surreptitiously and paradoxically reintroduced *metaphysics* in the conclusion. But it is a terribly inhuman metaphysics, an atheistic metaphysics in which mind is sacrificed to matter, freedom to the determined, man to things. This is no doubt what Engels called Marx's "subjective whims."

What should be our attitude as Negro Africans to this dehumanized humanism, to this deterministic subjectivism that negates the truly concrete subjective emotion? This is what I shall try to indicate. But first a word to explain the notion of *Negro African.* It is a fact that West Africa is inhabited not only by Negroes. Whether "marginal Negroes," like the Peul and the forest-dwellers, whether north Sudanese, south Sudanese, Guinean, or Sylvestrian—they are blacks.[14] Along with them, there are Berbers: whites. We do not deny this. On the contrary, the Mali Federation is proud to be a multiracial nation and even prouder to have integrated the cultural contributions of the Berbers, even of the Arabs. I should simply like to note that the whites— Berber-speaking Tuareg and Arabic-speaking Moors—are "marginal whites." As a Mauritanian political leader, himself a Moor, told me: "The Moors are Berbers with a high percentage of

Negro blood." Thus we are African Negroes with an admixture of Berber blood, as the French are Gauls of mixed Nordic and Mediterranean blood. On condition that we accept this contribution of Berber blood and culture—and we do accept it—we can call ourselves Negro Africans, understanding that this is only an approximation. In fact, Negro-Berbers would be more accurate.

What should be our attitude toward this Marxian humanism? I answer, first, that we should not betray its fruitful contributions when faithfulness to it can only lead to lucid transcendence. But West Africans are prone to betray it in both theory and practice, through blind allegiance.

In theory, one betrays Marx by using Marxian dialectics as it stands, without changing a comma. For this is reasoning twice in abstraction, the surest way to miss reality. We must not tire of repeating: Dialectical materialism is born of history and geography; it was born in the nineteenth century in Western Europe. Conceived in that milieu, it was essentially designed to analyze and transform it. Marx often affirmed this. The proof is that today, in those same countries, scientists and philosophers, writers and artists, while assimilating Marx's methodological contributions, have gone beyond, shaded, and enriched them to penetrate realities no longer of the nineteenth but of the twentieth century.

And what of Asian or African realities? The Israelis, like the Chinese have been able to find their Asian road to socialism adapted to the spirit and realities of their native soil. Theirs are exemplary efforts to inspire us. West African realities are those of underdeveloped countries—peasant countries here, cattle countries there—once feudalistic, but traditionally classless and with no wage-earning sector. They are community* countries where the group holds priority over the individual; they are, especially, religious countries, unselfish countries, where money is not King. Though dialectical materialism can help in analyzing our societies, it cannot fully interpret them. It did not even do so (nor does it now) in Europe, where we are witnessing a vigorous religious reawakening. Even in "Holy Russia," there is a resurgence of spiritual forces, with the defeat of false "socialist

* The French word is *communautaires*. [TRANS.]

realism," which, provided peace is preserved, we can anticipate in the near future.

Therefore, we would betray Marx by applying his method like a veneer to West African realities. We would betray him even more if we were to apply but not integrate European political, economic, social, and cultural organizations here, whether that of West or East, of liberal parliamentarianism or "peoples' democracy." This would strangely betray Man, as well as *Negro-African*—I mean *Negro-Berber*—humanism.

From a false theory, from a methodology which is inapplicable to the object, only *im-materialism* can result, insofar as matter is identified with the concrete: Only an *in-humanism* can result. In fact, the double abstraction just noted leads us in the first place to consider man *sub specie aeternitatis*. And man of all times and all places is no longer man but simply a mental image. For one can grasp man's permanent features only through his historical, geographical, and ethnic background. And the Negro, like the Berber, did not appear during the prehistoric era, not until the Neolithic Age, about the fifth millenium B.C. In the second place, the abstraction consists in seeing, under a black or copper skin, Marx's man in Africa, the European in the Negro or Berber—and classes struggling to conquer purchasing power in a mercantile world presented as an ideal of civilization.

How can one fail to realize that, in these conditions, *alienation,* far from being corrected, will be singularly aggravated? For the alienation of the Negro Berber does not stem from Negro-Berber capitalism, nor even from European capitalism. Nor does it stem from the class struggle. Rather, it results from the domination of one country over another—or rather, of one ethnic group over another. Here, political and cultural domination, colored by racism, is fused with economic domination.

Hence, for us, Man is not without a country, nor is he without a color or a history, a fatherland or a civilization. It is West African man, our neighbor, exactly defined in time and space. He is Malian, Mauritanian, Eburnian, Wolof, Targui, Songhai, Hausa, Fon, or Mossi. He is a man of flesh and blood, nourished on milk, millet, rice, and yams. He is a man humiliated for centuries, less perhaps in his nudity and hunger than in his skin and civilization, in his dignity.

Without this analysis, it is vain to define the program of the PFA or any African party. Unless one bears in mind the two realities of our present situation—the colonial fact and our cultural heritage. I know only too well that History, in its inexorable march, has reached the foot of the colonialist Bastille, that it is beginning to undermine the crumbling outer wall. Every republic in Black Africa can take its independence whenever it deems the moment opportune. Nevertheless, the sequels of colonialism remain and we must absorb and transcend them. As for our West African civilization, however charred it may be by the fire of conquest, it is now becoming verdant once again in the springtime of a new era, even before the first shower of Independence.

Our task is clear, with regard to the present and to the past— colonization and traditional civilization, the history that we have lived. We must emerge from our alienation to build a new state. Political, economic, and social disalienation, once again, are all prerequisites of cultural disalienation. Contrary to the notion of numerous African politicians, culture is not an appendage that can be lopped off without damage. It is not even a simple political means. Culture is the precondition and the goal of any policy worthy of the name.

What would be the use of raising the living standard of our masses without a rise in the standard of culture? What good would it do to increase purchasing power only for the comfort of belly and backside: to buy parasols and sunglasses, even automobiles, refrigerators, washing machines, and the like? What would be the advantage, unless we occupy our leisure by creating works of art to provide spiritual nourishment for our people? In my opinion, sport can be a work of art, like the cinema, radio, television, the theater, the novel, and poetry, sculpture, and painting, the dance and music. . . . I remind you that, in northern Sudanese countries with a single rainy season, people worked only during the four months of that rainy season. The other eight months, they were busy with social activities—I mean cultural activities—living in communion, by and within the community with other men, their brothers, more precisely, with the solidary forces of the entire universe: the living and the dead, men and animals, plants and pebbles. I am not saying that in the twentieth century it is unnecessary to reduce artistic activities for the benefit of political and economic interests. In the final analysis, all these activities are social, therefore cultural. Culture is inside and outside, above and beneath all human activities: It is the spirit that animates them, that gives a civilization its unique style.

In our return to our cultural roots, and particularly to the Negro-African method of knowledge and comprehension* of the world, we cannot reject European methods, but we also cannot forget Europe's lessons in building a nation, the socialist state. For the reasons discussed in my *Report* and, first and foremost, for historical reasons. We are now living the final stage of world unification through interdependence. Thus, though our humanism must have West African man as its major objective, it cannot, without peril, end with West Africa, not even with all of Africa. An effective humanism must be *open*; it obviously excludes not only *Malianism*—since we are not only Malians here assembled—but also nationalism and pan-Negroism (I do not say *Négritude*), pan-Africanism and, with greater reason, pan-Arabism. The one "Pan-ism" that meets twentieth-century requirements is, I dare say, pan-humanism—a humanism that includes all men on the dual basis of their contribution and their comprehension.

We shall make this salutary effort of reflection and construction if, in re-studying colonialism, we succeed in placing it in the historical process of world and African unification. Let us stop denouncing colonialism and Europe and attributing all our ills to them. Besides being not entirely fair, this is a negative approach, revealing our inferiority complex, the very complex the colonizer inoculated in us and whose accomplices we thereby are secretly becoming. It is too easy an alibi for our own laziness, for our selfishness as intellectuals, for our failures. It would

* *Con-naissance* and *ap-préhension* in the French. [TRANS.]

be more positive for us and our people to analyze the colonial fact objectively, while psychoanalyzing our resentment.[15]

Examined in historical perspective, the only fair perspective, colonization will appear to us at first glance as a general fact of history. Races, peoples, nations, and civilizations have always been in contact, and therefore in conflict. To be sure, conquerors sow ruin in their wake, but they also sow ideas and techniques that germinate and blossom into new harvests. Europe did not lose from the Roman conquest, nor did India from the Aryan conquest, nor the Middle East and North Africa from the Arab conquest.

The latest colonization, that of Europe over the world, was the work of the Renaissance. It stemmed from a social surge; it was stimulated and achieved by the confrontation of revolutionary ideas and techniques. It sprang from the humbling of the feudal landed gentry by monarchical centralization, and especially from the emergence in cities and communes of an intellectual and commercial bourgeoisie. Under the urging of this rising class that would later wage the French Revolution, the mind was freed and invented new techniques. It pushed God back toward heaven, de-sacralized the world and opened it fully to the European's feverish quest. The Renaissance was bourgeois and atheistic, mercantile and materialistic; it bore the seal of one essential aspect of the European mind. Thus it was iconoclastic, destructive of civilized values. But when examined more profoundly, on the level of universal history, the sanguinary event rises to the plane of an Advent; it is Revolution. Any revolution worthy of the name is, however, an upsurge of consciousness, consciousness of oneself and of others. I would say consciousness of the world, like the earlier great revolutions of Christianity, Islam, and Buddhism; and, like the subsequent French Revolution and capitalism, which were mingled within it, the Renaissance was a conqueror. But it exported not only merchants and soldiers; with professors, physicians, engineers, administrators, and missionaries, it also exported ideas and techniques. It not only destroyed, it built; it not only killed, it cured and educated; it gave birth to a new world, an entire world of our brothers, men of other races and continents!

When placed again in context, colonization will appear to us as a necessary evil, a historical necessity whence good will emerge, but on the sole condition that we, the colonized of yesterday, become conscious and that we will it. Slavery, feudalism, capitalism, and colonialism are the successive parturitions of History, painful like all parturitions. With the difference that here the child suffers more than the mother. That does not matter. If we are fully conscious of the scope of the *Advent,* we shall cease to inveigh against it; we shall be more attentive to contributions than to defects, to possibilities of rebirth rather than to death and destruction. Without the deaths, without the Arab and European depredations, no doubt the Negro Africans and Berbers would by now have created more ripe and more succulent fruits. I doubt that they would have caught up so soon with the advances caused in Europe by the Renaissance. The evil of colonization is less these ruptures than that we were deprived of the freedom to choose those European contributions most appropriate to our spirit.

As Arabia had before, Europe brought us virtues to fill the void she had provoked, seeds to be sown in the ashes of the devastated lands. With the development of the sciences, she brought us more efficient techniques than those at our disposal; these enabled us to build new cities on the ruins of the conquest. Like Arabia, by ruining the old Negro-African *animism,* which was not without value, it proposed to us a religion more attuned to contemporary values. Indeed, like the marabouts,* even more so than the marabouts, the missionaries were iconoclasts, destroyers of values. With this difference: that Islam, with its horror of imagery, has done more damage to cultural values, and Christianity, with occidental materialism, did more harm to moral values. (To speak only of Christianity, the best of the Christians —a Georges Gusdorf or a François Mauriac—have deplored certain methods of evangelization and the fact that the missionaries followed and sometimes preceded the merchants and soldiers. There is a seamy side to every human enterprise.) Nevertheless, Islam and Christianity gave us spiritual values as substitutes:

* Moslem holy men. [TRANS.]

more elaborate religions, more rational or, to repeat, more attuned to the present age. Once we have chosen them, it is our task to adapt these religions to our historical and sociological conditions: It is our task to *Negrofy* them.

To summarize on this point, *Independence* and *nation-building* require, first, along with *self-determination,* freedom of *choice.* We acquired this freedom with the Constitution of October 4, 1958. They also require the proper choice: in terms of West African, of our own, and of world realities. It is a question of placing our nation not only in the Africa of today, but also in the *Civilization of the Universal* yet to be built. The latter, as I like to repeat, will be a symbiosis of the most fecundating elements of all civilizations. In this perspective, we shall begin by returning to our West African sources—Negro-African and Berber—to imbibe there deeply. This presupposes a prior inventory of our virtues and *defects.* With this as a starting point, we shall make our own choices.

In truth, we have already made them. We have chosen the reconstruction of the former West African Federation and we have chosen independence in the multinational confederation with France. Furthermore, we have chosen as a means of realizing this the *African Road to Socialism.* Finally—and this is the purpose of this lecture—we have a choice to make in our final option. Everything in "scientific socialism" is not to be accepted, especially its *atheistic* materialism—I do not say its dialectical materialism. For the major contradiction of Marxism is that it presents itself as a *science,* whereas, despite its denials, it is based on an ethic. I have said that if historical development inevitably leads to socialism and Communism, why worry about it? In the name of what is our participation in this movement required? And how can one pass from *being* to *duty* except in the name of a transcendence of religious origin? For us, socialism is a *method* to be tested in contact with African realities. It is basically a question, after choosing lucidly, of assimilating our choices. To assimilate is to transform foods that are foreign to us, to make of them our flesh and blood—in a word, to *Negrofy* and *Berberize* them. This brings us back to Negro-Berber humanism; we must integrate the Negro Berber in his material determinations by transcending them in the name of certain spiritual values. For it is the spirit, in the final analysis, that judges and transcends the material determinants that have formed it. *Priority* of matter, if you will, but *primacy* of Spirit.

Toward a Strong Federal Democracy

Having defined the prerequisite of cultural independence and the aim of our policy, which is the realization of a West African humanism, we must now attack the *concrete* problems that arise in the construction of the new state. The latter can be reduced to a word or two: It is a question of building a great Negro-African, or, as I have said, a Negro-Berber nation.

Let us return then to the concept of Nation. I shall begin by recalling that the *nation* is not the same as the *fatherland*. It is not based, like the fatherland, on the natural determinants, such as race, language, religion and civilization. I know that all these help to form the nation and that the ideal nation would be one that coincides with the fatherland. In this regard, the creation of Mali has been facilitated by a series of fortunate facts:

1. Eighty per cent of the Malians belong to the Northern Sudanese sub-race.

2. The same Malians speak languages that are classed in either the Senegalo-Guinean or Nigero-Senegalese groups.

3. They live in the same North Sudanese civilization.

4. As early as the Middle Ages, as early as the era of the Great Empires—Ghana, Mali, and Songhai—they had rejected tribalism by transcending racial and religious quarrels. Islam, at that time a minority religion, was at first tolerated; today it tolerates the others.

Despite this example, the Nation, essentially, does not coincide with the fatherland. What makes the Nation, is a *common will for a life in common*. Generally this common will stems from history and the environment. Yet the history of the past sixty years has grouped us in the former French West Africa. It has taught us to know each other, to quarrel with one another, certainly, but also to appreciate and love one another. We could not reverse the current of history without risk of drowning. We

all recognized this these last few months. It is no accident that
the former Federation of French Equatorial Africa is being re-
formed as the Confederation of Equatorial Africa, no accident
that a *rapprochement* is in the offing between Mali, the *Entente,*
and Mauritania.

Now the question of a unitary state or a federation arises. We
shall not evade it, for it is the crux of the national debate. Inasmuch as it has been posed for almost one hundred years, by
socialism—first in 1863, in Proudhon's book *Du principe fédéra-
teur*. Lenin takes up the problem in his article, "The Right of
Nations to Self-Determination,"[16] where he often refers to Marx.
"An enemy of the principle of federation," Marx accepts it in
certain cases. For him, the essential factors are the "interests of
the proletariat" and "social development." The problem is thus
practical, not theoretical. The solution to be proposed must result
from the political, economic, and social analyses of a given situation. Lenin adopts the same position: It is, in short, for political
reasons—vast expanses of territory, differences of race, language,
religion, and civilization—that the U.S.S.R. has been organized
as a federation of autonomous republics. Theory, however,
insofar as it expresses a principle of universal validity, is not
entirely absent from Lenin's work. In a note to this article, he
writes:

> By the way, it is not difficult to see why, from a Social-Democratic
> point of view, the right of "self-determination" means *neither* federa-
> tion *nor* autonomy (although, speaking in the abstract, both come
> under the category of "self-determination"). The right to federation
> is, in general, an absurdity, since federation is a two-sided contract.
> It goes without saying that Marxists cannot place the defence of
> federalism in general in their program. As far as autonomy is con-
> cerned, Marxists defend not "the right to" autonomy but autonomy
> *itself,* as a general, universal principle of a democratic state with a
> mixed national composition, with sharp differences in geographical
> and other conditions.[17]

As will be noted, Lenin's thought is always subtle because it is
dialectical.

Of all this, we need retain only the essential. The problem of federation is a practical one for us as well. We shall retain, first, the idea of "free disposition" or, to use a fashionable term, "self-determination." It has more than a theoretical aspect. One cannot forcibly unify states that do not wish to be united. As a matter of fact, there are practical difficulties involved in realizing a great unitary state. Even in the most favorable instance, that of Senegal-Sudan, the dominant African language is not the same; for fifteen years the elites have been formed by different, if not antagonistic, political parties. But, above all, for sixty years, Senegal and Sudan have lived under different political regimes that have separated them instead of bringing them together, creating different mentalities in each place. The geographical, ethnic, cultural dissimilarities are even greater if one compares Mali with the other states. And another factor, an important one, is added: distance. All these differences, not to say oppositions, have crystallized into territorialisms that it would be useless to deny and that cannot in any event be eliminated for several decades. Even more serious, inside the same state, there are antagonisms that have not yet disappeared. This, fortunately, is not the case with Mali.

That, then, is our *situation*, which compels us to keep the federal structure. This is less serious than it first seems. On close, factual examination, the contrast between a unitary, decentralized state and a federal state is a false antinomy. They amount to the same thing, more or less—the difference is a matter of form, not of substance. The contradiction can and must be overcome and resolved! It is a matter of reconciling the need for a single direction to draw up the political program and method with the need for local control. The majority party will have the political conception and direction. The federal government and the federal assembly will direct foreign affairs. Whence the necessity for a strongly centralized party. The assemblies and governments of the federated states will control local affairs. The one is hardly less essential than the other, for reasons of principle and practice. Democracy requires us to start from the foundation, the masses; the popular will must first be expressed by the base, and the responsibilities, both economic and political, must be exercised there. This is what made us urge decentralization in

Mali as far as the federated states. On the other hand, too great centralization engenders *bureaucracy*: abstraction, where red tape is substituted for the realities of the native soil and theory replaces practice. Excessive centralization is France's misfortune. The Soviet Union recognized the danger and renounced the errors of Stalinism. Likewise most of the great modern nations, along with the U.S.S.R., the U.S.A., India, Brazil, Canada, and West Germany.

Viewed in this manner, the contrasts among our states and our peoples can be fruitful, provided they are exploited to advantage. They are the juices and saps that rise from the roots to the common trunk and the branches. This is the new blood that circulates throughout the entire body of the nation. These are the raw materials that feed the factory and leave it as finished products. The essential, once again, is that there be a head, a political direction that thinks, that has the initiative and control, that receives documents and suggestions to be transformed into plans and directives.

Democracy, I said in the chapter heading. Various European politicians, complacently accepting for definite purpose the declarations of certain African leaders, proclaim that democracy is impossible in Africa and, more generally, in underdeveloped countries. It would be wrong for us to listen to these white sirens. What good is our independence if it is only to imitate European totalitarianism, to replace external colonialism by domestic colonialism? *Dictatorship of the proletariat?* That is simply gargling a formula: There would have to be a proletariat and a capitalism "at war" in our countries, to use Marx's language. In our Negro-Berber society, as we have seen and cannot repeat too often, there are no classes at war, but only social groups struggling for influence. Tomorrow they will be at war with one another unless we are careful, if we allow the intellectuals—liberal professionals, civil servants, employees, and even laborers—to form a class that oppresses by misleading peasants, shepherds, and artisans. To prevent this, political parties and governments must be vigilant. Foreign capitalism is another problem that we shall discuss in the next chapter.

It is at this point that the question of the *opposition* should be raised. The opposition, necessary at first glance, must pursue the same goal as the majority party. This is to prevent social groups from hardening into antagonistic classes. Its role is precisely to be the conscience of governments and majority parties. Since the political and trade-union leaders are intellectuals, the temptation of the majority party is to favor the intellectuals against the peasants, shepherds, and artisans. On the other hand, the opposition is tempted to place itself, under the pretext of ideology, at the service of the foreigner. As you know, the opposition parties are teleguided from abroad: from certain African and European states. Their admitted objective is to subvert Mali. The duty of the PFA and of the governments of Mali is to adopt laws and measures to forestall this subversion, and to apply them with maximum rigor. On this score, all indulgence would be weakness, or rather, treason against the nation.

If we are to proscribe the single Party, does that mean that we should renounce the Unified Party and despair of rallying the opposition to our national ideal? No one could contend, no one in the PFA does contend this. And this is one distinction between Mali and other states of former French West Africa.

Because our positions are just, we can rally the opposition to them. You know what they are: to reconstitute the former federation on truly federal bases; to establish a new situation where there will be neither victor nor vanquished, neither pilot-state nor satellite, where the less poor will be solidary with the poorer. Our goal is also to lead this new federation to independence. We are not to blame if all the states have not joined the Mali Federation, if they are not all attaining independence at the same time. Our third objective is, to form, with the proclamation of independence, a multinational confederation with France, a *Commonwealth à la française*. In the previous chapter, I emphasized the fact that colonization is an historical event. It contributes more than errors and destruction; it is a *Revolution*. Like any revolution, it brings positive substitute values; it destroys in order to reconstruct. Our task is to integrate, to assimilate the complementary values with our own to make new blood. This is exactly the meaning of the multinational Confederation.

The justice of our position and the effectiveness of our program have enabled us to win 80 per cent of the votes in the elections of February and March, 1959. Since then, we have been able to attract a part of the opposition; all of the opposition in Sudan. The case of Senegal is a strange one; it can be explained historically. Here there was a long practice of parliamentary democracy similar to that of the Third Republic, with all the egotism, distorted verbalism, and contradictions that implies. It is amusing to hear the PFA attacked by those very persons who advocated "an African community before any other," those who demanded "negotiations" with France for the creation of a "multinational Confederation." The Senegalese opposition shows the cloven hoof—in other words, its selfish preoccupations—when it specifies as a condition for party unification "the sharing of responsibilities"—meaning ministerial portfolios. This is the opposite of democracy and socialism. The people are not deceived when they term these maneuvers "You-get-out-so-I-can-get-in-Independence."

The case of the opposition is different in Mauritania and the *Entente*. It is apparent that the governments of those states—except for Mauritania with her special problems—first obeyed a divisive maneuver designed in France. We know the role played by Soustelle in this operation. Obviously, the *Entente* states do not constitute a federation and are neither equal nor solidary. It is equally obvious that the opposition there does not enjoy the freedoms that exist in any democracy. This justified the policy of the opposition, which was almost wholly that of the PFA.

But things have changed. Now Mauritania and the *Entente* States are preparing, like the states of former French Equatorial Africa, to follow the Malian path to independence, if not to socialism. They now want to build an African Community with us (they avoid mention of a federation). A new situation, a new method. To adapt to this new situation, the opposition, sections of the PFA, must change its tactics—I do not say its program. Since the policy of the governments and majority parties is no longer negative, the attitude of our sections must be positive.

It will be, if they agree to collaborate loyally in the realization of the new objectives to the extent that these go in the direction of nationhood and the African community.

A coherent policy, effective because it is dynamic, consists of a few key ideas. As I stressed in my *Report,* contrary to what Marx and even Lenin thought, the coming of socialism, even of communism, could not relegate to the museum of history such aspirations as nationhood and independence, and such universal values as liberty, equality, and fraternity. The national idea is today the most solid reality of the twentieth century. The Russians and Chinese themselves, in becoming Communists, do not become less Russian and Chinese. They are perhaps more Russian and Chinese than anything else. Along with their great historic figures, they have exhumed and exalted the permanent values of their national civilization, of their race. Internationalism will be built only from the starting point of national realities, even from the realities of the fatherland. But internationalism, or better still, the Civilization of the Universal, must be built by transcending nations.

The renovated Community, the contractual Community surpasses the Malian nation in the sense thus defined. We have maintained, with certain modifications, the horizontal solidarity that links us to French-speaking African states. We must extend this solidarity vertically to Europe and to America, the daughter of Europe; horizontally to all Africa, even to Asia. This will be our positive contribution to the construction of the Civilization of the Universal.

But first to Africa, where we live and where the overwhelming majority of the inhabitants are Negro Africans and Arab Berbers. Immediately the problem of the United States of Africa arises. We shall not dodge this problem any more than we have evaded the others. We shall examine it with complete objectivity, without mincing words. Like President Bourguiba, I think the United States of Africa is not something to be achieved overnight. I am all the more free to say so because I was one of the first to propose it. About ten years ago, at the Consultative Assembly of the Council of Europe, Ousmane Socé* and I signed the draft of a resolution calling for the creation of the United States of Africa. But, once again, this will not be realized tomorrow.

Several factors oppose it. The first is that *continentalism* is a kind of self-sufficiency. Rejecting interdependence and collaboration, continentalism is, like every autarky, an impoverishing factor. We cannot dismiss the other continents, especially Europe and America, without increasing our relative backwardness. At the last Pan-African Conference in Tunis, there was talk, for example, of organizing an African Common Market. Have we weighed sufficiently the difficulties of this project? African economies are more competitive than complementary. Then too, we spend our time appealing to the *solidarity* of developed and underdeveloped countries, the rich and poor. Are not these appeals inconsistent with a tendency toward economic self-sufficiency? The second reason for the difficulty of the project is our lack of realism, our wordiness. We vote resolutions but do not implement them. If these resolutions were more realistic, we could perhaps begin to apply them. The third reason is that the actual deeds of independent African governments contradict their pan-African declarations. As soon as independence is acquired, most African states, still afflicted by European viruses, begin to secrete a conquering imperialism. They argue over their present borders, claim portions of neighboring territories, maintain in their countries, at considerable expense, emigrants and shadow governments or, in other countries, subsidize fifth columns in their service. I do not see how one can possibly create the United States of Africa if one starts by disuniting the states of the continent, if one does not begin by respecting their integrity and their frontiers.

It would be wiser to begin at the beginning: It would be more ethical and more realistic to recognize the equality of the African

* Ousmane Socé Diop, now Senegalese Ambassador to the United States, was named delegate to the Consultative Assembly of the Council of Europe in 1949. A former Minister of Planning, he has written several novels and short stories. [TRANS.]

States and at the same time to respect their frontiers, however artificial they may be. All borders are artificial, even in Europe. They have been traced by history. To those who invoke history to support their territorial claims, one can always answer by invoking more history. Mali is in a good position to maintain this policy, founded on ethics and historical realities. The right bank of the Senegal River was detached from this territory in 1920—"temporarily," the decree said—to be joined with Mauritania. It was not until 1943, I believe, that the Hodh was separated from Sudan. In the spirit that I have just described, Mali has abstained from claiming these two provinces.

Though Marx underestimated national realities, he rightly stressed international realities. African socialism must embrace and reconcile these two aspects of the same realities, which are both summed up in human solidarity. Considered from this angle, the problem of the United States of Africa becomes clearer. It is a question of being at once realistic and human; it is a matter of uniting Africa gradually, by making it a continent open to other continents. This opening will be facilitated by the maintenance of vertical solidarity that both the Commonwealth and the renovated Community propose. Our reasoning joins that of Ambassador Panikkar of India. In an article published a few years ago in *Preuves,* entitled "A l'Ouest de New-Delhi," he stated:

> Since Burma left the Commonwealth when she became an independent Republic it was generally conceded that India also would break her ties with Great Britain after adopting a republican constitution. To the surprise of most persons foreign to India and Great Britain, the new republic preferred to remain in the Commonwealth.

In this article, the Ambassador enumerated his country's reasons: As a member of the Commonwealth, India would occupy a more important place in the family of nations; she would obtain economic and technical assistance from Great Britain; finally, she would more firmly assure her cooperative links with Europe.

Toward a Community Society

In this chapter, I shall tackle neither economic and financial problems nor the cultural problem. My aim here is rather to

attempt to define an ideal society that will integrate the contributions of European socialism with our traditional values.
This integration is necessary since our society today, in 1960, is
neither the Negro-Berber society of the Middle Ages nor that of
contemporary Europe. Our present society is in fact an original
one, economically and culturally mixed, with African and European contributions. In *Le nouvel esprit philosophique,* Gaston
Bachelard appropriately observes that a new method is always
necessary to meet a new situation. This is the case here.

For the moment I shall leave aside the Berber society to limit
myself exclusively to the Negro African. That will facilitate the
analysis. Moreover, Negro Africans are the immense majority
of the West African population. On the other hand, Berber
society does not differ greatly from the pastoral society of the
marginal Negroes.

Maurice Delafosse, the great French ethnologist, describes
Negro-African society as "collectivist."[18] This is easily said, but
it would be more accurate to distinguish Negro-African society
from the collectivist society of European Communists (although
nowhere in Europe, not even in Russia, is there an authentic
collective society). This is so true that the Soviets describe their
society as "socialist," reserving the epithet "Communist" for the
final phase of their evolution. Judging from the liberal evolution
now delineated in the U.S.S.R., we may assume that the Communist society will always remain an ideal, never to be attained.
Not that I condemn the liberalization of the Soviet regime, quite
the contrary. I simply note the fact and that it is the norm.
Human nature has its exigencies that finally prevail when historical conditions are favorable. Raising the standard of living
and culture has its exigencies, one of which is freedom.

To return to the distinction between Negro-African and collectivist European society, I would say that the latter is an
assembly of individuals. The collectivist society inevitably places
the emphasis on the individual, on his original activity and his
needs. In this respect, the debate between "to each according to
his labor" and "to each according to his needs" is significant.
Negro-African society puts more stress on the group than on the
individual, more on *solidarity* than on the activity and needs of

the individual, more on the *communion* of persons than on their autonomy. Ours is a *community** society. This does not mean that it ignores the individual, or that collectivist society ignores solidarity, but the latter bases this solidarity on the activities of individuals, whereas the community society bases it on the general activity of the group.

Let us guard against believing that the community society ignores the *person,* even if we believe it neglects the individual. The individual is, in Europe, the man who distinguishes himself from the others and claims his autonomy to affirm himself in his basic originality. The member of the community society also claims his autonomy to affirm himself as a *being*. But he feels, he thinks that he can develop his potential, his originality, only in and by society, in union with all other men—indeed, with all other beings in the universe: God, animal, tree, or pebble.

Starting from this definition of the Negro-African community society, we can consider the special questions posed by the existence of distinct social groups in our West African society. This comprises three large sectors: (1) members of the liberal professions—lawyers, doctors, pharmacists, notaries, to whom we may add the merchants; (2) the wage earners—government officials, employees, and laborers; and (3) the peasants, shepherds, fishermen, and artisans.

These groups are less differentiated than in European society. First, because of our general underdevelopment and our democratic system of scholarships, a person passes easily from one group to the other. Moreover, the physicians and dentists, if not the pharmacists, are almost all government employees. It will be good to maintain this situation. On the other hand, the federal state will have to control the activities of the bar and of the notarial services. As for the merchants, most of them are small shopkeepers who present no immediate social threat. The danger would be that, instead of getting rich, they become poorer and poorer because of foreign capitalism and their lack of organization. Here again, it will be up to the state concerned to encourage them to unite and cooperate. This the state can do, and we shall see by what means.

* *Communautaire* in the French. [TRANS.]

The question of *capital* still remains. The problem is that this capital is not national but comes from developed countries. For this reason, it cannot be purely and simply nationalized. Several factors prevent it. In addition to legal difficulties, the nationalization of foreign capital would risk provoking international conflict, with which we have nothing to do. But above all, it would entail the loss of our international credit and prevent other investments, which are vital. Here we must be realists, test our imagination, and invent new methods of development. Suffice it to say that our problem is less one of nationalizing capital than of effectively orienting it to help our harmonious development. The state is well prepared for that. First of all, there are taxes. We shall simply take care not to "kill the goose that lays the golden eggs." The African states that claim to be the most socialistic are careful to tread this path cautiously. Otherwise, unemployment and poverty result. Secondly, our agreement for economic and financial cooperation with France enables us to channel credit. Finally, there is the possibility of creating national credit banks. All these means, none of them negligible, will make it possible for us to guide our economy toward effective poles of development, to socialize it harmoniously for the greatest benefit of our rural and urban masses.

Let us return to our social groups which, I repeat, are not *classes*. I have mentioned the liberal professions. Though they are the most highly educated, their members are not the most influential, either politcially or economically. The situation of the wage-earners, who are grouped in trade unions, is quite different.

I shall begin by paying tribute to the *Negro-African labor movement*. It was organized even before the liberation. It began at once to fight on both levels: political and economic. It played a most vital role in Black Africa, in *our own* liberation, of which the other Liberation—that of 1945—was merely the prelude. It produced the best political minds in Black Africa. Despite or because of these past services, trade unionism must be reconverted to a new and more precise idea of its proper function and tasks. Because today there are well-organized political parties that represent the whole nation on the federal political level, trade unionism must return to its natural role, which is primarily to defend the purchasing power of its members.

The great mistake of the unions, especially those affiliated with the UGTAN, is that they have not reflected sufficiently about the meaning of the *Loi-cadre*,* they have failed to understand it, and to realize that henceforth relationships between the trade-union movement and politics would be different. On the occasion of the referendum of September 28, 1958, their error was that they tried to replace political parties in an essentially political area. This mistake was repeated in Senegal at the beginning of 1959, when the UGTAN tried to influence the legislative election in March in favor of the foreigner, by provoking a political strike. The result, of course, was a new labor-union split and the weakening of the labor movement. These setbacks were studied by the most conscientious trade unionists and influenced their conversion.

Let us in our turn think about them, by referring to the Marxian conception of trade unionism. For Marx, economic relations, underlying social relations, are the motivating forces of history—especially in the mercantile, materialistic, capitalist system. In this system, the working class, because it is the most alienated, is the most conscious. Its task is to make the economic revolution by means of the political revolution. In Marx's opinion, the two revolutions are inseparable. This connection between the political and the economic justified the two-pronged struggle of Negro-African trade unions before the *Loi-cadre*. Negro-African society was intellectually, technically, politically, and therefore economically dominated by European capitalism —French capitalism, in our case. Although our situation was not exactly that of France, it was incumbent on the Negro-African labor movement to assume all the responsibilities of the *quasi-nation*. The date was 1944; at that time Negro-African political parties did not exist, except in Senegal. With their appearance in 1945, the situation began to change. The political revolution

---

* The Enabling Act. This law, voted in 1956, provided certain advantages, such as universal suffrage, to French African territories, but it also contributed to their balkanization, by dividing up French West Africa and French Equatorial Africa in semi-autonomous units. [TRANS.]

made a new start in 1957 with the autonomy of the territories proclaimed by the *Loi-cadre*. From then on, it was no longer incumbent on the unions, but rather on the political parties, to assume the totality of national responsibilities. From that moment on, the unions should have reconverted themselves to their natural role of defending professional interests. This reconversion after the victory of the proletariat is implicit in Marx's thinking. In actual fact and in all the Communist regimes, the reconversion has taken place after the proletarian revolution. Because it represents the totality of the interests of the masses and nation, the *Party* plays the major role of direction and control.

The need for reconversion of the labor movement is even more obvious in our Negro-African, Negro-Berber situation. Taking the example of Senegal, the most industralized state with the largest percentage of government employees, I note that there are only 100,000 wage-earners, representing scarcely 10 per cent of the working population. Without violating the most elementary rules of democracy, they could not speak for the entire population, which only the majority party could legitimately represent. In fact, this party comprises 85 per cent of the population.

Does this mean that trade unionism must change, selfishly, into an agency for grievances? I think not. As the best educated and therefore the most conscious group, the wage-earners must transcend their own group interests and their strictly professional preoccupations. Placing themselves on a higher level, they will embrace all the interests of all social groups and, first, those of the underprivileged: the peasants, shepherds, fishermen, and artisans. They will remember that in Mali the annual per capita income of these underprivileged groups is about twenty times lower than that of the wage-earners. They will readily concede that the living standard of the wage-earners can be raised only in proportion as that of the underprivileged rises, along with the national income. The conclusion to be drawn from this reflection is that the unions will adopt the general political program of the majority party and the governments. Furthermore, it is essential that this program—political, economic, social, and cultural—be truly national.

The National Confederation of Mali Trade Unions, just

formed in Dakar, has understood this. In closing the Constitutive Congress of the Confederation, Alassane Sow summarized its major goals in these words: "Abandoning all negative considerations, you have pledged to support a single and identical ideology: the construction and progress of independent Mali." It could not be better put. Apparently the reconversion is complete, though I fear not entirely so.

There are two reasons for this. The first is that adherence to the National Confederation to a Pan-African Union was rejected only after a long and dramatic debate. Independence cannot be divided. One cannot combat European, French colonialism merely to replace it with African colonialism. The imperialism of certain independent African states where the unions are in fact only satellites of the majority party removes all doubt of the danger of the Pan-African Union. There is no national independence when the most enlightened and influential social group is directed from abroad. The second reason for our apprehension is inspired by a sentence in the Resolution on Doctrine and Orientation: "The National Confederation of Mali Trade Unions considers itself absolutely engaged as a united force in the fight for our emancipation and well-being, and advocates its participation in the *management* of economic and social affairs, not simply as a consultant organization, but as *responsible* [My italics]." Here we are at the heart of the debate. As I noted earlier, the wage-earners constitute less than 10 per cent of the active population. To entrust them with control of the nation's interests, even if this were limited to economic and social affairs, would violate the rules of democracy: it would deny the existence of the state. I realize that here one will invoke the Marxian theory of the "withering away of the State." Even in Communist regimes, this theory has not resisted practical experience, for it is precisely in those regimes that the state is strongest. Men are not angels. To the extent that the individual is liberated by a rise in his standard of living and cultural level, the modern state, confronted by the increasing complexity of its problems, is obliged to reinforce its powers in order to fulfill its tasks. Nor is it pertinent to insist on the major role that the best educated and most conscious social group must play in the nation.

To grant privileges to the educator is to grant them to intellectuals or, more specifically, to the budding bourgeoisie. In Black Africa, however, government employees and even laborers are bourgeois in comparison with peasants and shepherds, fishermen, and artisans. It is a crime to call them *proletarians.* The role of the intellectuals and the trade unions is one of *counsel,* not of *control.* The majority party and the governments must consult them in their committees and study commissions. No more, no less. The unions will be better advised to create and manage cooperatives for purchase and consumption, which they have always neglected to do in Black Africa.

Let us have the courage to proceed with our self-criticism. I am speaking as a trade unionist. To entrust the control of state affairs to the unions would be to risk repetition of former mistakes. In the past, the unions naturally have been concerned more with defending their members' interests than those of the *quasi-nation.* The defense of these common interests and those of the most underprivileged groups was and still is incumbent on the state and the majority party. Though the annual income of the peasants, shepherds, and fishermen has risen since the liberation, this is less attributable to the unions than to the political party, for the simple reason that most members of the party are peasants, shepherds, and fishermen, not to mention the artisans and shopkeepers. The enlightened interests of the parties and nation requires that the underprivileged groups no longer be neglected as they were under the colonial regime. It is no longer possible to equalize African salaries and those of the metropole. On the contrary, they must be scaled in accordance to the national income, in line with the income of the underprivileged groups. To increase the latter's income is at the same time to increase the national income and to permit higher wages without risking disequilibrium and stagnation. Therefore, wages will not be lowered, but rather blocked, starting this year. This will enable us to utilize the savings thus realized for productive investments in the infrastructure, agriculture, cattle-raising, fishing, and handicrafts.

The problem of coexistence and harmonious development of social groups leads me to speak now about the Africanization of cadres. Once again, the question is not whether to Africanize the cadres in the government service; it is rather how to do so. Africanization of the cadres is linked to the notion of independence. In principle, the government workers of an independent state should be nationals of the state. But this principle is not always observed in a state belonging to a confederation. In Great Britain, for example, citizens of the Commonwealth or nationals of the dominions can be employees of the British Government. The same will probably obtain in France, in the transformed Community. Here it will be incumbent on the independent African States to settle the question by law. Our difficulty lies elsewhere, in the fact that we lack competent upper cadres.

How can we solve this contradiction between principle and fact? That is the whole problem. We agree that it is especially serious if we consider that the goal to be attained is not to serve special interests, to promote Samba or Demba, but to serve the general national interests by assuring a regular, efficient government service. To Africanize *at a discount,* by placing incompetent employees in posts requiring experienced workers, is to retrogress, to introduce anarchy, waste, and inefficiency in the government service, and to deprive us of the means of a modern state. Let us look around: The independent African states that most loudly proclaim their anticolonialism have escaped the contradiction only by appealing to the United Nations and to the foreigner, and by paying more dearly for the technicians on loan. Thanks to the cooperation agreement with France, our good fortune is that we have at our disposal technicians who rank among the best in the world and who are familiar with our problems. We would betray the national interest to deprive ourselves of this technical assistance. It is not a question of refusing the aid offered us at lowest cost but of choosing judiciously the most competent technicians for the positions to be filled. We must also abstain from an anachronistic racism with regard to those technicians.

Does this means that we should renounce Africanization? Not at all. To repeat, the problem is to determine which jobs to Africanize and how to Africanize. We must distinguish, as the Mali governments have done, between administrative and technical posts. In Mali, all the top posts, with exceptions that prove the rule, are now in African hands. Africans have taken over the positions that require initiative, direction, and control; they are responsible for the observance of the laws and of the general party directives. Officials in the General Administration suffice for this, provided they have experience in administrative affairs and a satisfactory political orientation. Nevertheless, the ideal will remain the administrator who has received appropriate juridical preparation in our National School of Administration.

The problem of the technical positions is quite different. One cannot put a nurse in the place of an elementary school teacher, or an elementary school teacher in the place of a professor of Latin or the latter in the chair of a professor of Arabic. Each to his own job, obviously. Let us rid ourselves of our complexes and ask France for all the technicians we need. Morocco and Tunisia, who are as nationalistic as we, invite hundreds of French professors and even elementary school teachers each year. And they refuse neither judges nor engineers nor physicians nor midwives nor nurses.

But the real problem is the *training of African cadres*. Our governments are working on this. At the moment, we are training enough minor and middle cadres. To have the upper cadres that we need, we must first broaden the base of our recruitment by developing secondary education. And we will not develop this until we train more African professors. Our second objective must be to prepare more technicians who meet international standards: engineers, physicians, veterinarians, judges, and also— along with researchers—financiers and economists. Most of these are being trained in the great scientific, technical, or administrative schools. Already France has reduced the age limit required of our students who wish to enter these schools. She must do more and organize similar competitive examinations for the students of the Community States for all these institutions.

I am not straying from the *African Road to Socialism*. Socialism is essentially the transformation of the economic relations between men, and the transformation of economic structures themselves. This requires the development of sciences and techniques and therefore the training of scientists and technicians.

It is a question of liberating the mind of all routine, of all scholastic prisons—including those of dogmatic Marxism—while developing productive forces at the same time. Socialism is a perpetual spirit of investigation and freedom; it is an *education* ever to be renewed.

Conclusion

The other day I was reading a trade-union newspaper pompously entitled *Le Prolétaire*. The editorial spoke of the profundity of UGTAN views. I thought I was dreaming. As if the UGTAN had not weakened the trade-union movement for the past two years by its lack of realism, its inability to analyze our *situation,* and its repeated failures. The editorial advocated social security. The founders of *Le Prolétaire* forget one thing: Their average monthly wage is about 36,000 CFA francs, which is higher than the per capita income of the inhabitant of France, whereas our peasants and shepherds who make up 90 per cent of our population earn less than 2,000 CFA francs. Are not the latter the true proletarians? As far as social security was concerned, our trade unionists were not curious enough to inquire who would finance it. Yet that is the first question. The second is to know, not whether the insured would receive money and how much, but whether they would really receive medical care and whether their children would get a free education. The best social security is that which provides medical care and instruction. This is the system that exists today in Mali: The one thing now needed is to perfect it. As for unemployment allowances, in addition to the expense involved, the most obvious result would be to depopulate our rural areas and increase the number of urban unemployed. In that way one would create, out of whole cloth, a wretched, ignorant, and embittered *proletariat*. Instead of suppressing the class war, one would artificially institutionalize it.

That is the classic example of that betrayal of scientific socialism which made Marx say in a letter to Engels that he (Marx) was not a "Marxist." Socialism does not reign in a Kingdom of Utopia or Demagogy. It is the objective analysis of the current social situation in a given country. Above all, it is the choice of the most effective means to transform that situation by resolving contradictions. No one denies that the methods and means recommended by Marx are still valid to the extent that Europe has formed our society and that nineteenth-century realities subsist in the twentieth century. But philosophical reflection has progressed during this century and scientific methods along with knowledge—techniques also. First and foremost, however we may be influenced by Europe, our realities are not identical. To remain faithful to socialism means that, facing these new realities, we must choose new methods, new techniques, and new means—the most modern and most perfected ones. In a word, West Africa, and especially Mali, must be a vast workshop for research. Our task is nothing less than to give the world the example of a new country creating a new civilization in tune with Africa and with the twentieth-century world.

The Theory
and Practice of
Senegalese
Socialism*

A t the outset, I should caution you against a certain distrust
of theory, which I have detected in a number of political
leaders of the UPS (Senegalese Progressive Union). This
is a dangerous error. The founders of socialism rightly stressed
the importance of theory. As Engels said, "A nation that wishes
to remain at the summit of science cannot manage without theoretical thought."[1] They even held that theory is the *sine qua non*
of effective practice.

Why? That is the first question to answer. There is no human
action without theorizing, outside of instinctive movements and
acts of folly. These are called acts rather than action, since action
implies the carrying out of an intended scheme of acts coordinated by thought. In fact, language, being a structured ensemble of concept-words or simply of signs, is already theorizing.
The same is true of thought, which is expressed by language. But
theory is always born of practice, of *praxis*, as the Marxists say.
It is the abstraction of practice, in that it retains only the common
data, which it sets up as a law for future action. In other words,
the theoretician retains from past experience only the lessons that
enable him, on the one hand, to know the object and, on the
other hand, to act more effectively in and on the future.

---

* Speech delivered at the Seminar for Political Cadres of the Senegalese
Progressive Union, November–December, 1962.

Science offers us the most pertinent example of theory. The scientist is the man who, in a certain field, studies the reactions of a given object—a thing or a living being—to various situations. Of these reactions, the scientist notes only the common characteristics, which, in a second movement of abstraction, he will express as a law. For example, when biologists about a century ago wanted to study heredity, they took plants of different species and varieties, crossed them over several generations and noted the results of these crossings. From these, they formulated laws, the most famous of which was Mendel's law. The essential fact that Mendel perceived was that certain characteristics were dominant or recessive. Whence he was able to deduce his law, in other words, to define the fundamental rules on which today geneticists, cattle breeders and farmers, educators, and politicians base their practical action.

You will have noticed that I have taken the word *theory* to mean law rather than hypothesis, since the latter is merely a law to be verified and explained in the light of the facts: experience or experimentation.

And yet theory does not only stem from practice, it corrects and perfects itself by practice. This is the dialectics of theory that Marx and Engels stressed. In research on heredity, the botanists led the way, because plants lend themselves more easily than animals to experimentation. Even Mendel's law was not a definitive formula. To understand the whole reality, all realities, the experimentation had to extend to the greatest possible number of plants and animals. It was especially necessary to seek the why of the law. One finally found it in the genes of the chromosomes which, enclosed in the nuclei of the cells, transmit hereditary traits. Subsequent research has produced new facts. We know today that changes in the species are due not only to crossing but also to the influence of the environment. We also know that hybrids are indefinitely fertile in the human species. This enables Teilhard de Chardin to proclaim *homo sapiens* as the common origin of all human races. You can guess the practical consequences that this has for the philosopher, the moralist, the politician.

It is helpful to complete these general considerations by studying the problem of technique. Technique has been defined as "applied science." Thus, technique is still theory but already practice. In fact, in the course of their respective developments, theory and technique on the one hand, and practice and technique on the other, have always been related.

To illustrate this, I shall take the example of the most modern Senegalese agriculture: the peanut culture. Agricultural technique is an ensemble of body movements, extended by instruments working by animal or automotive traction when not directly moved by hand or foot. The totality of these movements makes up agricultural technique to the extent that it is thought out and then coordinated in action. Hence it is at once theory and practice. Theory in the sense that it rests on scientific knowledge, born of experience or experimentation; practice in that contrary to pure science, its nature and objective are the transformation, not merely the disinterested knowledge, of the real.

Thus the modern peanut culture, which requires precise knowledge of various scientific disciplines: climatology, botany, soil science, and, in a general way, physics and chemistry. Scientific techniques, such as seed selection, plowing, fertilizing, sowing, hoeing, weeding, reaping, garnering, must be applied. A certain number of instruments must be used: the plow, the seeder, the hoe, the wheelbarrow. These instruments still represent applied science, whether in their manufacture or their use. As Gaston Bachelard observes, "The instruments are only materialized theories. They come from phenomena that bear, everywhere, the mark of the theoretical."[2] Throughout this essay we shall see that theory and practice, at each stage of their development, are linked, leaning one on another as they progress.

I. Scientific Socialism

If, at the close of World War II, we chose socialism as a political doctrine, it was because, to make our anticolonialist struggle effective, we needed a practical method that would be the appliction of a certain theory. For socialism is at the same time theory and practice. Engels defines it as a method, not as a dogma.

Dogma is "a point of doctrine established or considered as a basic truth, axiomatic in a religion or philosophical school." By its religious or philosophical accent, dogma is the opposite of scientific law. Etymologically, it is an opinion. It transcends facts by explaining them instead of being explained by them. At best, to the extent that dogma claims to stick to facts, it considers them *static*. This is what the term metaphysics expresses; its literal meaning is "beyond the physical, beyond the concrete."

As for method, the dictionary gives two principal meanings. It is either a "series of steps that the mind takes to discover and demonstrate the truth," or preferably "a series of reasoned steps to reach an objective, in any field whatsoever."[3] In other words, method is at once theory and practice, more precisely: a theory, not disinterested, but conceived to be applied toward a definite objective. From this viewpoint, the search for truth itself could not be considered entirely disinterested. The author of the *Discourse on Method* (Descartes) explained this in a letter dated February 27, 1637: "It [method] has more to do with practice than with theory." Thus, method is a *technique* that itself is only the sum total of the intellectual and material, theoretical and practical processes of an art or trade. In sum, like technique, it is the synthesis of diverse means employed to attain, effectively, an end. It is this end that prescribes the choice of means and their synthesis.

And so Engels was perfectly right to define *socialism* as a method: at once theory and practice, but, first of all, *praxis*. I shall try in this first part of my presentation to define: (1) the object of the scientific socialism of Marx and Engels; (2) its finality (ultimate goal) and its objectives (primary aims); and (3) its method and *technique,* or means.

Object

First, its object. Socialism is essentially *politics,* that is, an art of governing men of a given society by organizing their relations harmoniously. Thus, the object of socialism is not the economy, as too many Marxists now believe, but concrete, living man, in his totality, body and soul. "It is rather symptomatic of the present-day confusion of values," writes Lefebvre, "that an 'absolute economism' has been attributed to Marx, whereas his thinking proposes, essentially, to transcend economic man."[4]

If Marx and Engels stressed the economy, it was for practical reasons, because man is defined, or better still, is fulfilled by his practical activity as a producer-consumer. It is through this activity that the founders of scientific socialism want to attain nature and, first of all, man. If they protested against "the classical economics" taught prior to their time, this was because its laws are appearances that mask man's being. What they wanted to do was to penetrate beneath the fetishized economic laws, "to penetrate," as Marx said, "the real and intimate totality of the relationships of production in bourgeois society"—what they were actually witnessing in the mid-nineteenth century in Western Europe.

Their theory, or more exactly their dialectical method, was not elaborated without reference to the real. In their early philosophical works, Marx and Engels attacked logic, even Hegelian logic. (It is significant that Engels' *Dialectics of Nature* is a posthumous work.) The two thinkers blamed Hegel for having formulated a simple theory that was divorced from practice and from the concrete—in a word, from life. As a matter of fact, for Hegel, dialectical logic was "the absolute foundation of all things." According to him, it was form that determined content, mind that constructed matter, reason that built nature—that is to say, being, with which nature coincides. Marx analyzed this theory as follows: "All things being reduced to a logical category, and every movement, every act of production, to method, it follows naturally that every aggregate of products and production, of objects and of movement, can be reduced to a form of applied metaphysics."[5]

Thus Marx and Engels began by seeing men in society, empirically—eating and drinking, finding lodging and clothing, and, above all, working. They began by describing and analyzing human *praxis* before theorizing about it, by discovering laws in the phenomena of life before formulating them. The political philosophy of Marx and Engels is, primarily, a phenomenology; it is materialism, but historical before it is dialectical.

Nevertheless, Hegel and his disciple Feuerbach did influence

Marx and Engels in their method of research. How true it is that the most empirical observation is seldom without a plan, without a rough outline of a theory! Defining the new spirit of geometry, Gaston Bachelard points out "that experimentation depends on a prior intellectual construction" and that "one seeks in the abstract the proof of the coherence of the concrete."[6] What is true of experimentation is equally true of observation, and *a fortiori*, what is true for geometry is equally true for sociology. After all, if Hegel concentrated on ideas, he no less sought their historical origin, their production: "Anyone who is even only slightly acquainted with his Hegel will be aware that in hundreds of passages Hegel is capable of giving the most striking individual illustrations from nature and history of the dialectical laws."[7] Hegel presents man as produced by his generic activity in a historical process but, at the same time, as alienated or dehumanized by the objects of his productivity.

But the idea of materialism came from Feuerbach, who openly rebelled against his master. Feuerbach's essential merit was that he stressed not the idea but man, not thought but the act, not consciousness of the object but the object of consciousness. Nevertheless, for Marx and Engels, Feuerbach represented a step backward from Hegel. He considered man static, in accord for all eternity with an unchanging nature. The genius of Marx and Engels is that remembering Hegel and assimilating evolutionism, they extended materialism to the dimensions of history.

It is time to observe how Marx and Engels, in their early works, discover and define man concretely, through his generic activity and his history. To these works we shall add Engels' *Dialectics of Nature*.

"Man is directly a natural being." "History is his natural process of genesis."[8] These two propositions express the two poles of Marx's and Engels' phenomenology, of their historical materialism. Man, the object of scientific socialism, is presented concretely, in his life, as object and subject, as a historical product of nature but producing, historically, nature and himself along with it. Let us explain this by leaning on Engels, who is clearer and more "scientific" than Marx. In *Dialectics of Nature*, Engels attempts a history of nature, a phenomenology that is a veritable *summa*, since it embraces almost all sciences: mathematics, mechanics, astronomy, physics, chemistry, biology, sociology. This encyclopedic effort recalls the work of Teilhard de Chardin, to whom we shall refer later.

For Engels, the point of departure, as far back in time as one can go, is nature, that is to say, matter endowed with certain concrete properties. In the midst of this nature, man emerged. Thus, the study of man as well as of nature must be made in time and in space. "In contrast to the history of man, which develops in time, there was ascribed to the history of nature only an unfolding in space." Man is not created once and for all from the outside, imposed upon an immutable nature. Like nature, he "does not just exist, but comes into being and passes away."[9] This is what the history of the so-called exact sciences, the natural and human sciences, reveals.

Starting from biology and leading up to sociology and psychology, Engels describes man's production. Relying on facts and using Hegel's dialectical method, he lets himself be guided by the evolution theory developed by Lamarck and Darwin. After affirming that "the innumerable classes, orders, families, genera, and species of animals" were created and developed by "continual differentiation,"—in other words, by mutations—he comes to man. "Man too arises by differentiation."[10]

Then focusing his descriptive analysis on man's development, Engels shows him progressively evolving in space and time, by the reciprocal action of hand and brain, tool and consciousness. Yet, the hand was unable to be extended by the tool, the brain was unable to express itself in consciousness without labor—that is to say, production, the veritable basis and motivating force of society.

The mastery over nature, which begins with the development of the hand, with labor, widened man's horizon at every new advance. He was continually discovering new, hitherto unknown, properties of natural objects. On the other hand, the development of labor necessarily helped to bring the members of society closer together by multiplying cases of mutual support, joint activity, and by making clear the advantage of this joint activity to each individual. In short, men in the making arrived at the point where *they had something to say* to one another.[11]

Recapitulating the process of man's formation, Engels concludes:

> First comes labour, after it, and then side by side with it, articulate speech—these were the two most essential stimuli under the influence of which the brain of the ape gradually changed into that of man, which for all its similarity to the former is far larger and more perfect. Hand in hand with the development of the brain went the development of its most immediate instruments—the sense organs.[12]

So men are grouped in society under the interacting stimuli of labor and speech, thanks to the hand extended by the tool, and to the brain extended by the senses. This society, a decisive phase of development consisting of reciprocal action and complementary activities among men, will give birth to civilization. What, indeed, is civilization but the adaptation of nature to man and of man to nature, man's domestication of nature and nature's rapid transformation of man? Transformation not only of the body, by improving man's lodging, clothing, and food, but also transformation of his thinking, by the quantitative and qualitative development of his brain. Here we are at the "critical threshold" of human evolution, as Teilhard de Chardin would say, for "the further men become removed from animals, the more their effect on nature assumes the character of a premeditated, planned action directed toward definite ends known in advance."[13]

Engels' analysis joins that which Marx had made in his early works and in Volume II of *Capital*. Marx had defined work as a "vital, conscious activity" and, consequently, voluntary, free, creative. This is what finally distinguishes man from the animal. "But what from the very first distinguishes the most incompetent architect from the best of bees, is that the architect has built a cell in his head before he constructs it in wax."

Were I to stop at this point, I would have presented man's evolution, according to Marx and Engels, as a continuous straight line, a unilateral movement, whereas it is discontinuous and ambiguous. It is made of advances, then backward steps, then greater strides forward once again; it is made of reactions between hand and brain, body and mind, man and nature, man and his products. In short, it is progress, but equivocal progress, an equilibrium that is quickly upset and ever to be re-established—in sum, a dialectic of life. To decipher and explain it, Marx and Engels introduce the Hegelian concept of alienation. One finds this in their early works, especially in *German Ideology*.

Paradoxically, alienation, which I would translate as disappropriation, stems from the progress of human society, from the development of the means of production and, consequently, from production itself. In primitive society—that of food gatherers, hunters and the first farmers—everything is held in common: tools, labor, and the products of labor. But with the perfecting and multiplication of tools, production increases and inspires new needs. Consciousness develops along with the brain, which invents new techniques—"spinning, weaving, metal-working, pottery, and navigation"[14]—and a division of labor, based on sex, age, and technico-professional groups. This is the beginning of industrialization, which will make a decisive leap forward with the invention of the steam engine. Meanwhile, man has passed progressively from the rural primitive community to feudal society, and from feudal society to mercantile society, to end up with modern capitalist society.

All these new social realities—development of tools and production, development of consciousness and needs, the division of labor—produce the state of alienation. It is in capitalist society that alienation appears in its most complete form and that we shall study it.

First of all, in production, in labor. Free in the peasant community, labor becomes forced in the factory, deprived of its living rhythm, without song, without joy. No longer is it the creative labor of the worker realizing his aim freely, in body and consciousness, by "fulfilling himself." Now it is work on the assembly line, imposed from the outside by the employer.

Alienation as well in the product. With the division of labor and the relative abundance of products, the latter are no longer the "fruits of labor," possessed in common by the community. They have become *merchandise*, possessed individually by the employer and put up for sale. An *exchange-value* has been substituted for their *use-value*; and we have passed from a community economy to a mercantile, capitalist economy; from collective ownership to private property. The products of labor no longer belong to the workers, but to the idle employer who has inherited the instruments of production. Those who have rented out their labor receive only a part of the price. The remainder, the surplus value, increases the capital, which belongs to the employer. This is the essence of the second alienation, of which there are two aspects. The worker's needs, increased by his labor and by the abundance of products, are not satisfied. But, above all, his products, transformed into merchandise, are reified. Taking on a *reality,* an independent artificial life—in the framework of what we would call the world market and world prices—they turn against the worker and provoke recurrent depressions, with their poverty and famine. . . .

As labor and the products of labor escape the worker and turn against him to dominate him, he loses his spirit. His only preoccupation now becomes the satisfaction of his material, biological, animal needs. He mistakes this satisfaction for life, for the end, whereas it is only the means. "The more the worker produces by his labor," Marx writes, "the more powerful the strange world of objects created by him looms before him, and the poorer his inner world becomes. . . . The working man no longer feels free except in his animal functions: eating, drinking, and procreating."[15]

So much for the worker. As for the employer, he increasingly relinquishes the actual management of the factory to the technicians. This allows him considerable leisure that he can devote to the development of his mind, of culture: religion, art, law, science. He can do this the more readily because all his animal needs have already been easily satisfied.

Because of the division of men into two hostile classes, resulting from the division of labor into material activity and intellectual or spiritual activity, into content and form, *into praxis and theory,* the spiritual forces, deprived of their concrete content and practical activity, function in a vacuum, *abstractly.* Taking on a new though abstract reality, and making a dialectical twist, these spiritual forces turn against the producers to dominate them. Thus, the ideas of the dominant class are artificially but concretely imposed on the working masses, the proletariat, as an *ideology.* . . .

Let us continue our analysis of *reification.* We shall examine it not from the exterior, in relation to the division of labor, but from the interior, in the creative activity of the producers or, more precisely, in the relation of *subject* to *object,* of *man* to *nature.*

As we have said, man is at the outset a "natural being." He is a product of nature, but an incomplete one, realized only *in* and *through* nature. He is a sum of biological energies and needs, a vital force tending toward the satisfaction of his needs. He is an active subject whose activity has indifferent nature as its object. A natural product, man becomes a producer thanks to the impulsion of his biological energies—instincts, tendencies, and conscience—which become *passion.* In fact, "passion is man's faculties striving to attain their object."[16] His aim is the realization of his *being.* Man exists only by his creative activity, only when he objectifies his being by creating products *in* and *through* nature. "Man affirms himself as a specific being in the elaboration of the world of objects. This production is his active life. Thanks to it, nature appears as his work and his reality."[17]

The generic, creative activity of productive man comprises three degrees that mark the progress toward *reification* or *alienation.*[18]

At the food-gathering phase, the phase of the rural community, man carves out in nature the objects of his activity, which he transforms into instruments and consumer goods with a use-value. Here, the object is immediately linked to the subject through the satisfaction of his natural needs.

But during the second phase, the perfecting of tools, the abundance of products, the division of society into classes, and the development of brain and conscience provoke the autonomy of products. Becoming *social products,* they forge new links between themselves and with the classes. No longer consumer goods, the products become *merchandise* and money. Men are no longer in direct, *immediate* relation with each other; they must pass through their products, which become go-betweens. Relations between things—merchandise and money—replace relations between men. More precisely, they mask the relations between individuals by transforming them into abstract social relations. In capitalist society, however, social relations no longer reflect the community effort toward the fulfillment of all the individuals by the common and total appropriation of products. Merchandise and money become *ends* rather than *means,* ends the antagonistic classes pursue in a struggle where man becomes a wolf to man.

In this situation of a mercantile, monetary society where man's products deny man, man must resolve the inhuman contradiction by transcending it—by suppressing not the products, but their *abstraction,* that is to say, their autonomy. For in one sense, the reified products concretely express the real life of men, their activities and needs. But man must appropriate and interiorize this reality of the products by deciphering the true relations among them and with him: not their *form* but their *content.* Only thus will man achieve the second stage of his development by integrating with social life.

Marx and Engels tell us that in this movement to integrate by deciphering and interiorization, man has created law, religion, ethics, and art. Like merchandise and money, these are products of man's conscious activity. "Religion, the family, the state, law, morality, science, art, etc.," Marx affirms, "are only *particular* forms of production and come under its general laws."[19]

The production of spiritual products, *ideologies,* therefore answers the need to transcend the second phase of production— the first phase of alienation—in which social products, detached from individuals, turn brutally against them, empty their activity of its content, and leave their material and social needs unsatisfied. To fill this void, ideologies are used. Their aim is the individual's appropriation of social products, the reunification of nature—subject and object—not only by this natural appropriation, but also by consciousness of it.

Ideologies—law, religion, ethics, art—as Marx notes in *German Ideology,* are always the products of the rising class when it is about to take over. And they are the truths of that particular *moment.*

The class making a revolution appears from the very start, merely because it is opposed to a *class,* not as a class but as a representative of the whole of society; it appears as the whole mass of society confronting the one ruling class. It can do this because, to start with, its interest is more connected with the common interest of all other non-ruling classes, because under the pressure of conditions, its interest has not yet been able to develop as the particular interest of a particular class.[20]

In the Middle Ages, the triumphant aristocracy established the notions of "honour, loyalty, etc.," whereas in the nineteenth century, "during the dominance of the bourgeoisie, the concepts of freedom, equality, etc." prevailed.[21] Hence, with each victory, the rising class humanized social products for a larger number of people by clarifying the relations between individuals and their social products, between man and nature.

Religion and art have conquered new domains of coherent clarity from the mystery of ignorance and contradiction—a spiritual function. Law and ethics have corrected morals on foundations more human because they are more just—a normative function. On the whole, consciousness (that is to say, theory) has gained in coherence, and praxis has gained in efficiency.

But ideologies are crystallized spiritual products. One usually says that mores precede laws, and that the latter merely confirm the former by fixing them. But the movement of history, evolution, soon transcended ideologies, and praxis soon outdistanced theory. As the concrete material life of man is transformed, his spiritual products, detached from this life, acquire their independence, just as material products had done earlier. Made to *serve* men, ideologies turn against them to enslave them. This was the new situation created by capitalist society in the mid-nineteenth century. Identifying with the capitalist class, the bourgeoisie no longer defended anything but the interests of an idle, futureless minority. Religion and art no longer expressed anything but false myths at the service of this class. Law and ethics codified the interests of capitalism.

We must transcend this third phase of production, this second alienation. How? By denying, once again, not the products themselves but the abstraction of them, insofar as these are products of man's generic activity. As a matter of fact, spiritual products represent man's legitimate effort toward "unity and self-reconciliation, tranquillity and salvation"[22]—and beyond that, toward the unity and reconciliation of man with nature. But for Marx and Engels, the error of ideologies is to set themselves up as absolutes, as fetishes, whereas they only express historical truths—partial, relative, transitory. Their major defect is that they seek unity—of man with the community, of man with nature—within a power foreign to man: in the products, not in the producer; in the object, not in the relation between object and subject; in theory-belief, rather than in the reciprocal action of theory and practice.

Once again, the suppression of the second alienation, the solution of these new contradictions, can be found only in creative activity, the practical and social activity of the producers, of individuals organized as a community. Thus, law and ethics, instead of translating a past moment of history and therefore of man, must translate the interests and struggle of the rising class: the proletariat "whose class objectives merge with the liberation of the whole man."[23] "For us," said Lenin, carrying Marx's ethic to its ultimate consequences, "there is no such thing as morality taken outside of human society; such morality is a fraud. For us, morality is subordinated to the interests of the class struggle of the proletariat."[24] Like law and ethics, art will also attain its true role as creative production, which is an effort by man—in both theory and practice—to express himself fully by expressing nature. As for religion, or God, Marx considers that if one returns to the true active subject, man, then the idea and therefore the mediation of God is useless, "for atheism is a *negation of God* and seeks to assert by this negation the *existence of man*."[25] Therefore, disalienation, by transcending the contradictions, and thus enabling man to realize his potential, can only be achieved actively and practically, consciously and socially.

It is only in a social context that subjectivism and objectivism, spiritualism and materialism, activity and passivity, cease to be antinomies and thus cease to exist as such antinomies. The resolution of the *theoretical* contradictions is possible *only* through practical means, only through the *practical* energy of man. Their resolution is not by any means, therefore, only a problem of knowledge, but is a *real* problem of life which philosophy was unable to solve precisely because it saw there a purely theoretical problem.[26]

This conscious, concerted, but practical activity, which suppresses the division of classes and harmonizes production to eliminate contradiction and opposition between man and his products or between man and nature, is what Marx calls Communism. Not crude Communism, which is only "sharing," but true Communism, "the real *appropriation* of *human* nature through and for man . . . as a complete and conscious return which assimilates all the wealth of previous development . . . the return of man himself as a *social,* i.e., really human, being." Then he gives us this definition: Communism is both humanism and naturalism; "it is the definitive resolution of the antagonism between man and nature, and between man and man . . . between freedom and necessity, between individual and species."[27]

Goal and Objectives

Twentieth-century man, especially the *prospector,* has rehabilitated the search for the *end.* Not only the ultimate goal—finality —but also the immediate goal, the objectives. This is what our compatriot, Gaston Berger, has done in creating *Prospective* as a science of the future, more exactly, as an *hypothesis about the future* (not so much the immediate future, amenable to the objectives, but the distant future). "*Prospective,*" he explains, "is especially the study of the distant future." And as this is studied in relation to man and his activities, it "compels the prospective searcher to pose the problem of ends." Not only is this a valid method for the man of action since "more or less consciously man acts toward some end," but the present potency of our means compels us to it.[28] Our first reaction to the fantastic success of the space flights is to ask: "To what end?"

And yet, Marx and Engels did not dwell on the problem of ends. Why? No doubt because their work remained unfinished; but, more surely, because scientific progress did not then permit them an accurate forecast of the future; even more surely, in my opinion, because of *praxis.* This is because the ends are multiple

—economic, political, cultural—and because they depend partly on the means at our disposal and on how we use them. "In fact," Berger observes, "means and end influence each other reciprocally, following a subtle, complex dialectic."[29] Marx had already said this: "The resolution of the theoretical contradictions is possible *only* through practical means, only through the practical energy of man."[30]

For Marx, determining the substance of the ends is a theoretical problem that will be resolved at the appropriate moment only by practice. What must be defined is the *how* of the ends and the situation in which they are realized. Thus, man's goal will only be realized by the recovery of his "human dignity"; in other words, the realization of real man can only be accomplished by man's appropriation of "his universal being in a universal manner"—the appropriation of his labor and of the material and spiritual products of it—therefore, of nature.

But man's alienation, as we have analyzed it, impedes this appropriation, which is man's ultimate goal. This alienation, in opposition to integration, Marx defines as follows: "Alienation is the opposition between *within oneself* and *for oneself,* between *consciousness* and *consciousness of oneself,* between object and subject, or the opposition between abstract thought in sensible reality, or of real materiality in thought itself." The general objective to achieve, in order to reach man's ultimate goal, is therefore the suppression of his alienation. This long-term goal is broken down into two more immediate objectives: political and economic.

The political objective has priority; it is treated by Marx and Engels in their political works. (From Marx we shall cite: *The Eighteenth Brumaire of Louis Bonaparte, The Civil War in France,* and *The Class Struggles in France.*) To destroy capitalism, the major instrument of alienation, a political revolution is first necessary, which will aim at taking over the power and apparatus of the state. For it is in fact because of this apparatus (bureaucracy, justice, army, police) that capitalism—along with the class structure, or the domination of one class by another— is maintained. The state supports its material apparatus by a class ideology, founded on religion, ethics, law, and even art. The take-

over will be accomplished by *violence*. "Force," says Marx, "will
be our road to revolution in most countries of the globe, because
one must resort to force at a given moment to establish defini-
tively the government of labor."[31]

The power takeover will be the work of the proletariat, organized as a party of the class and of the mass, of the workers.
This action, however, requires *theoretical* preparation and *practical* organization. These will be effected by the Party avant-
garde, which will endeavor, by the political, economic and sociological analysis of society, to make the proletariat *conscious* of
its situation, for this consciousness is the first condition of every
revolutionary *will*. But to carry over into action, this will must
be concretely organized into strategy based on strict discipline.

As soon as the Party takes over, it will establish the dictatorship of the *proletariat*—not a new arbitrary power, but, democratically, the power of the formerly oppressed majority that will
eliminate capitalism's contradictions, the sources of underdevelopment and injustice. The dictatorship of the proletariat is the
socialist state.

Before proceeding, it is pertinent to recall Marx's distinction
between *socialism* and *Communism*. Socialism is not yet Communism; it is the preparation for Communism, a temporary stage
on the road to Communism. Both entail a dual task—political
and economic—but of a different type.

Politically, socialism retains the apparatus of the state in order
to transform it, for the struggle has not ended. Neither the
bourgeoisie nor its instrument, capitalism, has yet been eliminated. This apparatus must be placed in the hands of the working elite; "democratically controlled organisms to direct industry,
trade, and agriculture, to develop the productive forces, and to
organize them rationally" must be created.[32]

Socialist planning provides this rational organization of productive forces, for their development and also for a more equitable distribution of their products. In socialist society, however,
the distribution depends not on the needs but on the labor of
each. This is the economic objective of socialism. Neither Marx
nor Engels goes into detail about planning. We find no project
in their works, but rather a definition and justification of plan-

ning—in Marx's *Capital* and especially in Engels' *Dialectics of Nature,* where we read: "Only conscious organization of social production, in which production and distribution are carried on in a planned way, can lift mankind above the rest of the animal world as regards the social aspect, in the same way that production in general has done this for men in their aspect as species. Historical evolution makes such an organization daily more indispensable, but also with every day more possible. From it will date a new epoch of history."[33]

Communism is politically and economically defined as the final liquidation of all the sequels of capitalism. The state as a political system "withers away" and is absorbed in society. From the mass of workers, the most capable individuals have emerged to organize and control the various economic and social sectors. Political activity disappears, lacking any object, since classes as such disappear. On the other hand, economic and social activities emerge, thanks to the prodigious development of the productive forces. This will be the age of abundance where each will receive according to his needs. Because the division of labor into manual and intellectual pursuits will have vanished,[34] and because the individual will merge with society, freedom will attain its plenitude. Each individual's natural talents will flower because they will have been developed in a rational manner; this is what constitutes *culture.* There, then, is *Communism* realized as the final stage of *integral man.* This, Marx concludes, "is the definitive resolution of the antagonism between man and nature, and between man and man . . . between objectification and self-affirmation, between freedom and necessity, between individual and species."[35] The contradictions of capitalism have been resolved, dialectically, by analysis and transcendence.

Method and Means

Analysis and transcendence. Here we tackle Marx's major contributions to contemporary civilization: his method (dialectics), inseparable from a certain conception of the world (materialism), and the technical and moral means of realizing the *Communist man.*

The exposé of the method and "conception of the world" of dialectical materialism* is not easy, and for two reasons. First, because it is complex thought, and secondly, because Marx did not explain it systematically "in a few dozen pages," as he had promised Engels he would in a letter dated January 14, 1858. Fortunately, we have at our disposal Engels' work on this problem, *Dialectics of Nature* (though it is incomplete), and also the philosophical work in which Marx criticizes Hegel's method while indicating its positive aspects.[36]

Let us begin with dialectics, which we shall distinguish from formal logic. We say "formal logic" because dialectics is also logic, if we understand it to be "the science of reasoning" or "the art of discovering the truth." Formal logic is that of the understanding, of common sense; it "seeks to determine intellectual operations independently of the experimental, peculiar, and contingent content of any concrete affirmation"[37]; it aims at clear, coherent reasoning and accordingly supposes that objects are stable and unchanging, and that the content shares in the form. Formal logic rests on the two principles of identity and non-contradiction. Examples: "A is A" and "A is not non-A" or "A is not B."

> So-called *objective* dialectics [Engels writes] prevails throughout nature, and so-called subjective dialectics, dialectical thought, is only the reflex of the movement in opposites which asserts itself everywhere in nature, and which by the continual conflict of the opposites and their final merging into one another, or into higher forms, determines the life of nature.[38]

Earlier, Engels had stated: "The laws of dialectics . . . can be reduced in the main to three: The law of the transformation of quantity into quality and *vice versa*; the law of the interpenetration of opposites; the law of the negation of the negation."[39] Thus, the dialectician can say at the same time: "A is A" and "A is not A," or "A is not B" and "A is B."

This deserves an explanation. "Objective dialectics" considers

* This expression is not Marx's.

external objects as they really are, in perpetual transformation, not as common sense sees them:

> The plant, the animal, every cell is at every moment of its life identical with itself and yet becoming distinct from itself, by absorption and excretion of substances, by respiration, in short by a sum of incessant molecular changes which make up life and the sum total of whose results are evident to our eyes in the phases of life: embryonic life, youth, sexual maturity, process of reproduction, old age, death.[40]

Absolute identity exists only in mathematics, which deals "with ideal objects." As soon as one renders a specific judgment— "the lily is a *plant*"; "the *rose* is red" one states a difference, a contradiction, for the predicate, or the attribute, is different from the subject.

Let us go further. Dialectical logic is that of reason. Beyond the form, beyond the principles and categories of understanding and of common sense, thought enters into immediate rapport with "the varied, changing content."[41] As the theory of evolution has shown, all things and all beings contain within themselves contradictory elements, the reciprocal action of which transforms some of them into things, others into beings.

Dialectical reason is thought that grasps not only the contradiction in the object, but the movement, by reciprocal action, of the contradictory elements. This movement consists of three terms, which we shall try to define. Every object contains two elements, "two opposing and necessary determinations."[42] Let us return to Engels' example, that of a simple cell that will become a man. "All progress that will lead up to man is effected by the constant conflict between heredity and adaptation."[43] When I say that this cell, or child, is "heredity"—first term—I limit and immobilize it by isolating it. Yet its nature is to be in relation to another object: to be a *relationship*. "In its determination as heredity, it is destined not to remain static."[44] When I deny that affirmation of "heredity"—second term—I also complete it, by pointing out that heredity is a partial and one-sided truth, since it neglects "the adaptation to the environment," but a truth nonetheless. My negation is therefore an affirmation. Which leads me to deny this negation. This third term—"the negation of the negation"—is the dynamic synthesis of affirmation and negation:

> The contradiction, which pushed each term beyond itself, snatching it from its finitude and inserting it in the total movement, is resolved. The third term unites and transcends the contradictions and preserves whatever is specific. Unity triumphs after a period of fruitful convulsions.[45]

Thus the third term is the *synthesis, unity*. In other words, it is the overcoming of contradictions, the becoming, the *future*. In this instance, it is the adult man, fruit of heredity and environment, more exactly, of the transcendence of them both. But, because it is a becoming, this third term contains the germ of new contradictions which must, in their turn, be transcended by the same dialectical movement. And so on. I could have chosen other examples: electricity, a chemical body, a social phenomenon. In any case, we would have again encountered contradiction and its transcendence. This is what Marx shows us in his analysis of capital. It is the movement I have explained here.

Dialectical logic does not destroy formal logic any more than the principle of contradiction destroys the principle of identity. Formal logic, we repeat, is that of common sense, made for objects isolated in space and time; it is the logic of a world simplified by abstraction. "Abstract identity, like all metaphysical categories, suffices for *everyday* use, where small-scale conditions or brief periods of time are in question."[46] As soon as we deal with the infinitely great or the infinitely small, with historical dimension or scientific activity, we must resort to dialectical logic. And yet, if we go to the heart of the problem, we discover that the one does not destroy the other. "Dialectical logic transcends static affirmations but does not destroy them. It does not reject the principle of identity; it gives it content."[47] What does this mean? It means that identity is the inner unity of everything, tension between the different poles, equilibrium always to be established over contradiction. Identity is the unity of contradictions whence emerges—third term—a new and higher being. This is the meaning of Engels' sentence: "Most natural scientists imagine that identity and difference are irreconcilable opposites, instead of one-sided poles the truth of which lies only in their reciprocal action, in the inclusion of difference *within* identity."[48] He had written earlier "that true, concrete identity includes difference and change within itself."

What we have just said about the principles of identity and contradiction could apply equally to other concepts of understanding or other "logical categories" on which reasoning and knowledge are based: necessity and contingency, cause and effect, positive and negative, the whole and the part, simple and compound. One could say the same of the types of activity of the understanding, or of forms of reasoning: induction and deduction, analysis and synthesis.

In my attempted definition of formal logic and dialectics, I have referred to Marx and especially to Engels. Also to Henri Lefebvre, the best French specialist on Marxism, and to his analysis of Hegel's dialectics as they are presented in Hegel's *Logic, Encyclopedia of Philosophy,* and *Phenomenology of Mind.* For, if Marx and Engels began by criticizing Hegel, they did not fail to pay him homage, especially at the end of their lives, and acknowledge their indebtedness to him. They reproach him for having considered dialectics as "forms of thought, logical forms which are detached from *real* spirit and *real* nature."[49] They accuse him of having deduced the laws of dialectics from the mind rather than from nature; of having maintained that the mind, with its forms and categories, created nature, the real world. For Marx and Engels, it was exactly the contrary: "It is from the history of nature and human society that the laws of dialectics are abstracted."[50] So spoke Engels. And Marx explained:

> My dialectic method is not only different from the Hegelian, but is its direct opposite. To Hegel, the life-process of the human brain, *i.e.,* the process of thinking, which, under the name of "the Idea," he even transforms into an independent subject, is the demiurgos of the real world, and the real world is only the external, phenomenal form of "the Idea." With me, on the contrary, the ideal is nothing else than the material world reflected by the human mind, and translated into forms of thought.[51]

This is the famous theory of the reflection or the copy on which is founded the "conception of the world," the Marxian

Weltanschauung, as the Germans say. In truth, the materialism
of Marx and Engels is a concept, a philosophical notion, a working hypothesis. "Matter as such," Engels notes, "is a pure creation of thought and a pure abstraction. We disregard qualitative differences of things by listing them as matter so long as
they exist bodily. Matter, as such, differs from existing determined matters by having no sensitive existence." This is the
abstraction of matter, considered as a substance, the essence of
the real world, that made Engels reduce it to motion, to energy,
the forms of which he is content to study. This is the abstraction that made him consider materialism as metaphysics. Marx's
treatment, I must point out, is more delicately shaded. In his
view, materialism is a working hypothesis that must be verified
by practice. "The chief defect of all materialism up to now
(including Feuerbach's)," he writes, "is, that the object, reality,
what we apprehend through our senses is understood only in the
form of the *object* or *contemplation*; but not as *sensuous human
activity,* as *practice.*" This is an observation of capital importance. For matter, here, is less the object than the practical activity—that is to say, the dialectics of subject and object: "the
practical-critical revolutionary activity." Thus Marx goes so far
as to speak of the "materiality" of "thought" and of its expression: "language."[52]

And so we are led to explain briefly the theory of knowledge
of Marx and Engels: their gnosiology. "If we know the forms of
motion of matter (for which it is true there is still very much
lacking, in view of the short time that natural science has existed), then we know matter itself, and therewith our knowledge
is complete."[53] Marx says almost the same thing:

> The method of presentation must of course differ formally from the
> method of inquiry. The method of inquiry has to appropriate the
> material in detail, to analyse its different forms of development, to
> trace out their inner connections. Not until this preliminary work
> has been effected can the movement as it really is be suitably de-
> scribed. If the description is successful, if the life of the latter is
> reflected on the ideal plane, then it may appear as if we had before
> us nothing more than an *a priori* construction.[54]

The importance of this gnosiology must be stressed. It insists on: (1) the mobile, evolutionary character of reality; (2) its character of objectivity; (3) its implicitly contradictory character, since it is in motion—more precisely, the "inner relations" of its contradictory elements; and (4) the originality of each object studied, which is grasped by the study "in detail" of its matter.[55] It must be noted, however, that here the two socialist thinkers forgot to insist on the activity of thought, which is to comprehend the object through the categories of the understanding and in a reciprocal action of subject and object.

With this method of dialectical materialism—overturned and then restored after Hegel and Feuerbach—Marx studied, analyzed, and reconstructed the life of capital. As we have seen, he chose capital because it was the bourgeoisie's method of production and distribution in the mid-nineteenth century; because the maintenance of its system alienated the masses and kept them in a situation of economic, social, and cultural underdevelopment; because the system had to be overthrown in order to liberate the masses by disalienating them; because it was first necessary to analyze and explain the situation to make the proletariat conscious of its alienation. Today, one might expect that Marx would have proposed some other system in its place. We have seen that he had recommended, *grosso modo,* a long-term goal and immediate objectives. We must still discuss the technical means that he proposed to attain these objectives.

These technical means are implicitly contained in *Capital.* They are summed up in planning, which is to prevent crises of relative overproduction. Planning evidently presupposes, as we have already indicated, the dictatorship of the proletariat in politics and the suppression of capitalism and nationalization of means of production in economics.

Let us not forget that *Capital* is an unfinished work. If Marx had had time, he would probably have indicated in detail the conditions to be met by effective planning. We can, however, list these conditions by referring to Engels' *Dialectics of Nature,* especially its introduction and the chapters on the role of labor and biology.

For Engels, as for Marx, planning—"the conscious organization of social production"—is required by the contradictions of the capitalist method of production, as analyzed in *Capital*. The major contradiction is described as follows: "Increasing overwork and increasing misery of the masses, and every ten years a great collapse."[56] This basic contradiction has two causes. The first is that "the profit to be gained from the sale becomes the sole motivation" of capitalist production: immediate profit. The second is that, through ignorance, the capitalists do not foresee the long-term consequences of their method of production. "And then surprise is expressed," Engels observes, "that the more remote effects of actions directed to this end turn out to be of quite a different, mainly even of quite an opposite, character."[57]

Thus, the general objective of efficient planning must be the suppression of that contradiction. It must have the effect both of developing maximum production and of distributing production equitably among the workers by developing consumption. In other words, planning must realize the following conditions of a new type of *socialistic* production and distribution: the elimination of private property and profit by nationalization; collective ownership of the means of production that will correspond to the collective production—cooperation—division of labor; (2) development of scientific research and the creation of a true prospective, as Berger would say, so that knowing in this way "the more remote natural consequences at least of our more ordinary productive activities," we shall then learn "to master them";[58] (3) establishment, on these bases, of a true economic development plan, which will harmonize the development of means of production (infrastructure and heavy industry) and means of consumption (processing industry and rural economy); and (4) distribution of the value of products according to the labor of each worker.

As a result of all this, planning is as practical (realization of the plan) as it is theoretical (preparation of the plan on the basis of a scientific inventory).

To the totality of coordinated technical means just described as planning is added the totality of coordinated spiritual means which one calls ethics. In an article entitled "The Communism of the Future," Zakaria Ibrahim, of Cairo, affirms: "In truth,

Marxism thinks more about creating a 'new man' than about establishing a philosophical, political, or economic doctrine."[59] This statement is true insofar as Marx's philosophical, political, and economic doctrine tends to help man become a total man, by suppressing all alienations, in order to objectivize himself in nature or to integrate nature in himself. "Its premises," Marx writes, "are men, not men in any fantastic isolation or abstract definition, but in their actual, empirically perceptive process of development under definite conditions."[60] To realize themselves, men will therefore have to accomplish a political and economic revolution, which will be expressed by the *dictatorship of the proletariat* and by *planning*. But they cannot do it without being animated by a *conscious and practical revolutionary will*. It is in this will that one finds *ethics,* which is *at the same time theory and practice*.

Marxian ethics presents two aspects: negative and positive. It is a critique of past ethics, of religious ethics: Above all, it is the elaboration of a morality, of a new *ethic*.

In Marx's opinion, the moral codes of the past originally had a material basis, in the sense that they expressed the "conditions of existence" of the era. When the *rising class,* of which they were the expression and which presented them as universal values, congealed into a *dominant* class, these "moral codes always tended toward the fixation and immobilization of the society,"[61] and the rising class "proved them obviously false."

To understand the range and limitations of past codes of morality as well as the need for a new socialist morality, it is necessary to place them, like all other material and spiritual facts, in the evolutionary movement of history. "Religion, the family, the state, law, morality, science, art, etc. are only *particular* forms of production and come under its general laws."[62] As we have said, *religion,* the foundation of the great moral codes of the past—Christianity, to which we would add Islam—is an explanation designed to resolve contradictions between man and his products, man and his needs, real man and nature, a global attempt to solve these contradictions by intuition. Intuition, because sciences were then in their infancy and did not permit an exact analysis of these contradictions, technique being then rudimentary and incapable of providing effective solutions. Ethics was the application to life of intuitively posed rules.

Finally Marx came on the scene. Armed with an effective method—dialectical materialism—he made a pertinent analysis of religion and ethics. He showed their ideological superstructure, built outside of the real, taking on independent life and turning against man—in short, a second alienation.

Marxian ethics aims to suppress this second alienation, theoretically and practically. Theoretically, by recognizing in the facts "the production of man by human labor, thus the future of nature for man": in other words, by recognizing man's existence without recourse to "a being placed above nature and man." This is absolute atheism, "for atheism is a *negation of God* and seeks to assert by this negation the *existence of man*." Practically, by having man develop through the mediation of the proletariat, the rising class, the new class. "Every new class," Marx writes, "achieves its hegemony only on a broader basis than that of the class ruling previously." Moreover, "the struggle to be waged . . . aims at a more decided and radical negation of the previous conditions of society than could all previous classes which sought to rule."[63] The proletariat has a dual advantage: It is a majority, especially if the poor peasants unite with the workers, as Lenin will subsequently ask them to do; it also possesses an intrinsic strength, an unequaled power of negation.

Thus it behooves the proletariat to put an end to spiritual alienation by its practical action. It will do so by liberating itself spiritually from religious fetishism, by creating a new ethic with its own values, and by practicing this ethic. Assuming the destiny of the whole society, Marxian morality blends with the struggle and interests of the proletariat. "For us," Lenin will affirm, "morality is subordinate to the interests of the class struggle of the proletariat."[64] How can this class morality be founded on human values that are universal in scope? This remains to be examined. Once again we shall have to distinguish between theory and practice.

First, it is a matter of making a complete anthropological study of man—historical, biological, psychological—which will determine the objective conditions of his development, of his flowering into contemporary man. The anthropological *laws* of this human development will be posed as moral rules, for the *human fact* by its very nature has a human, moral value.

Having become rules, these human facts must be considered and *practiced* in the *prospective* of their becoming: They must be transcended. "Transcendence," Lefebvre comments, "means going in the direction of future evolution, toward total man. . . . Transcendence therefore implies an imperative of knowledge, action, and increasing realization."[65] I would be tempted to define transcendence as planning based on a scientific *prospective,* the aim of which is the political, economic, social, and cultural development "of the whole man and of all men." The moral code of this transcendence is a collective and individual discipline not only conscious and freely accepted, but also effectively applied.

II. Senegalese Socialism

Looking objectively and retrospectively at the doctrine or method of Marx and Engels, we shall not fail to be impressed by its scope and soundness. It is not only a method but a *doctrine,* a new vision of the future, a *Weltanschauung.* This is partly what causes its weakness, as we shall see. But its soundness rests on *dialectical logic* and most often, it will suffice us to carry this logic to its ultimate consequences in order to complete and, we dare say, to *rectify* the vision of the two socialist thinkers.

We shall thus be aided in this task by Marx and Engels themselves, and also by contemporary scientists and philosophers, such as Teilhard de Chardin.[66] Furthermore, we shall be helped by the theoreticians of *Arab socialism,* writing of a situation akin to our own, and, finally, by a return to our roots, to the values of *Négritude.*

Let me explain. Since the doctrine of Marx and Engels is presented as historical and scientific, I remind you that during the past century, history and science have advanced with giant strides. The social problem today is less a class struggle within a nation than a global struggle between the "have" nations (including the Soviet Union) and the proletarian nations (including the Chinese People's Republic), and we are one of these "have-not" nations. As for science, the discoveries since Engels' death—of relativity, quanta mechanics, wave mechanics, relations of uncertainty—have upset the materialist and determinist metaphysics of Marx and Engels.[67] Moreover, alongside of our investigations, there are those of Arab socialism, which we would be wrong to underestimate. I refer you to Nos. 18, 19, and 20 of the magazine *Orient,* which contain relevant articles on nationalism, socialism, and religion. The general theme of these articles is that the methodological and technical contributions of European socialism must be integrated with Arab nationalism, which is based essentially on Arab history and culture. Dr. Aal Dawahbi defines Arabism as follows: "An Arab is one who speaks Arabic, whose existence flows from the history of the people who speak that language." When the Arabs include religion among the elements of Arabism, they are careful to explain, as does Dr. Ahmed Fouad al Ahwani, that, "The religion we are talking about is not Islam alone; it is also the revealed religions which, born on this territory and emanating from a common divine trunk, separated into three branches."[68] To support this, he quotes several verses from the Koran, such as this one: "Believers, Jews, Christians, and Sabeans—whoever believes in Allah and the Last Day and does what is right—shall be rewarded by their Lord: They have nothing to fear or to regret." (2:62) Thus, like the Arab socialists, we shall integrate the contributions of European socialism with our nationalism, with the values of *Négritude,* defined as the common denominator of all Negro Africans, whatever their race, religion, or country.

Let us take up one by one the various divisions of our first chapter and examine them critically by referring both to contemporary science and history, and to our Senegalese, Negro-African situation. While doing so, we shall bear in mind our intention to examine them always from a dual point of view: theoretical and practical. We shall remember that "the resolution of the *theoretical* contradictions is possible *only* through practical means, only through the *practical* energy of man," that "their resolution is not by any means only a problem of knowledge, but is a *real* problem of life which philosophy was unable to solve precisely because it saw there a purely theoretical problem."[69]

Object

As indicated earlier, the object studied by scientific socialism is man, not immutable man, created at one fell swoop, but man as he evolves historically. Marx and Engels place him in history, but in a history explained by the natural sciences. "History itself," Marx comments, "is a *real* part of *natural history,* of the development of nature into man. Natural science will one day incorporate the science of man, just as the science of man will incorporate natural science; here will be a single science."[70]

Engels tried to explain this unified science in *Dialectics of Nature.* But at that time (about 1890) the great scientific discoveries mentioned at the beginning of this chapter had not yet been made. Teilhard de Chardin picked up Engels' project in the *The Phenomenon of Man,* invoking not only natural sciences, but also physics, chemistry, and even mathematics. Teilhard de Chardin had a twofold advantage: The great scientific discoveries had already been made; as a paleontologist, he was himself a specialist in natural sciences.

Let us return to Teilhard's method. It is dialectical—theory and practice—and based on logical coherence and practical fecundity, which the scientist uses as his criteria for truth. His study has man as its object, whence the significant title of his major work. Teilhard studies man not as a philosopher or theologian, but as a scientist, retaining only the facts, the phenomena. His volume, he explains, is "purely and exclusively . . . a scientific treatise. . . . The book deals with man *solely* as a phenomenon; but it also deals with the *whole* phenomenon of man."[71] Another aspect of his method is that, like Marx and Engels, he studies man in his evolution, his becoming. Evolution is his working hypothesis: an evolutionism perfected by a century of investigations. The phenomenologist is not satisfied to analyze and catalog facts: by revealing their movement, he tries to discover their meaning; the direction of their future develop-ment, their finality.

Thus Teilhard studies the biological and psychological history of man. He does not start with the Reformation and from the cell as Engels does[72]; he plunges beyond the Apparition of Man,[73] and of the cell—as far back as the atom that he decomposes. From the pre-life to the future, *survival,* he studies the phe-nomenon of man as it evolves from seemingly inanimate matter to the Omega point (God), while crossing the critical thresholds of the biosphere (life) and nous-sphere (thought).

Let us follow him, with the pre-life as our starting point. "Matter," Teilhard writes, "is constantly presented in the form of calibrated elements, larger and larger, but inevitably forming a multitude, on each level."[74] This is the phenomenon that he calls *corpusculization.* Thus an atom is formed by a nucleus and electrons, a molecule by a group of atoms, a cell by a group of molecules, and a living being by a group of cells. Like Marx and Engels, Teilhard starts with matter.[75] But it is not a metaphysi-cal matter, defined only as exteriority. He starts with a scientific matter scientifically analyzed.

But what is *corpusculization?* According to Teilhard, it is the effect of two other phenomena: *outer gravity,* which forces mat-ter to unite into planets and stars, and an *inner gravity,* which attracts toward the most improbable, the most complex com-binations.

After *corpusculization,* we must define *complexity.* What does Teilhard mean when he says that the second characteristic of matter is the complexity of the particles' association within the corpuscle? "Complexity," he explains, "is heterogeneity organized and, consequently, centered." It is an association *organized,* center to center, of different corpuscles into a larger corpuscle which itself possesses an organizing center. What makes the com-plexity of an association is the number of elements composing it—above all, "the number, variety, and contraction of the liai-sons (density) existing between these elements in a minimum of volume."[76] Thus, from the nucleus of the atom to the living being, we progress toward a greater complexity, as we pass through the atom, the molecule, and the cell.

At this point, it is pertinent to note one characteristic of matter that Teilhard strongly emphasized. Engels had already insisted on the transformation of quantity into quality and vice versa. After pointing out the transformation of qualities of matter in the immense (relativity) and the infinitesimal (quanta), Teilhard stresses it in the phenomenon of complexification of corpusculization. In the movement of complexification of matter, one progresses jerkily, passing through critical points, thresholds beyond which new properties of matter appear—such as life, and then consciousness. This is the *general law* of *complexity-consciousness*.

Having started from the atom nucleus, and having reached the cell, we are now, according to this law, on the threshold of life, of the *biosphere*. At a certain critical point of atomic complexification, life appears with its specific characteristics, which are *consciousness,* first in the form of instinct; then reproduction, and formation of species by mutation. (Mutations, the result of heredity and education—adaptation to the environment—add up to give birth to a new species or *phylum.*) Thus, *in the direction of more correlation and coherence, in the direction of greater complexity and consciousness,* the human phylum is born.

Man, like other living beings, begins by belonging to the biosphere. At the outset he is *Homo faber,* scarcely distinct from the ape. But he distinguishes himself from it none the less. In other animals, directed mutations—orthogenesis—lead to the transformation of a limb or of the whole body into an instrument."[77] In man, the hand is transformed, as Engels had noted.[78] But in man, Teilhard specifies, the transformation affects the structure of the limbs less than that of the brain, which not only increases in volume, but presents a more complex association of a greater number of cells. Man's brain attains a critical point on the axis of *complexity-consciousness,* whence *reflection* emerges. We are entering the domain of thought: the *nous-sphere*.

This nous-sphere, man's proper domain, comprises three stages: *reflection, co-reflection,* and *ultra-reflection.* Let us examine these one after the other.

Reflection is "consciousness to the second power." It is "man no longer merely a being who knows" but "a being who knows that he knows."[79] It is thought re-flecting (bending back) on itself, and thus multiplying its power. From that point on, man can think on a *universal* scale, in total space and total time. With this new instrument, man invades the entire earth. Human groupings—tribes, nations, races—spin social relations among each other, thanks to this physical presence and to *language*, the expression of thought. They weave "a continuous membrane of thought that encircles the earth."[80] This is the phenomenon of the totalization of the earth. In this first phase, man, by *practice*—Engels would say, by labor—invented *technique*. Technique is the fabrication of instruments separate from man's body, more numerous and better perfected than the hand. These instruments enable man "to construct the earth," to transform it into a second universe.

We have already reached the second stage: that of co-reflection. In the preceding stage, a new phylum of man had appeared: *Homo sapiens,* thinking man, from whom all present races descend. "The expansive convergence" of totalization is followed by the second stage, the "compressive convergence" of *socialization.* Since the planet earth is a closed surface and since men multiply, they are compelled to "adjust" lest they be "crushed."[81] To adjust by multiplying their social relations, by pooling their reflections, their instruments and techniques—above all, by cooperating to invent new thoughts, new techniques, new instruments to permit a better adjustment. That is *co-reflection,* the origin of socialization, that Teilhard likens to civilization. In other words, since the Renaissance and the great discoveries, since the beginnings of modern colonization, we have been living in the era of co-reflection.

But what is socialization-civilization? It is, the scientist answers, the organization of human relations, the reconstruction of the earth—of nature, Marx and Engels would say—for the promotion of a new *human* society. By "human society" we mean not one nation, one race, one continent, but all men without exception in a common effort of organization and reconstruction, of co-reflection.

Whereas Marx and Engels talked of economic infrastructure,

Teilhard again probes back to the *biological* and *psychic* roots of society. The biological roots can be summed up in one word: *heredity*. By the association of the genes of his two parents, every man born is the *synthesis* of two contributions. More exactly, he is a *symbiosis*: an aggregate of new qualities that is superior to the components. He is a *biological co-reflection,* making possible, by the effects of *combination,* higher forms of consciousness. All the races of man are, thus, more or less mixed. And Teilhard concludes with a thought that has tremendous significance: "In the final analysis, the most humanized human collectivities always seem to us to be the product, not of segregation, but of synthesis."[82]

The *psychological roots* of co-reflection are found in language, which is at once the instrument and product of co-reflection. Through language, we inherit the technical knowledge of the previous generation, which the present generation enriches before transmitting on to the next.

Those two elements are dialectically related. "The one (the biological roots), a material arrangement generating more psyche; and the other (the psychological roots), the awakening of a psyche that generates even more arrangement."[83] They have accelerated the process of socialization by gradually producing the symbiosis of different civilizations. This explains how, before our very eyes, the Civilization of the Universal is being built. Despite the Cold War, there exists today a common conception of the world, an identical way of feeling and judging things.

The organization and intensification of co-reflection carries us toward ultra-reflection, since thought is the attribute of man.* This upsurge toward *maximum-being*† results from four factors: technical development, scientific development, national development, and the development of international life.

From the foregoing, we can measure the progress realized in our knowledge of the *human phenomenon* since 1890, since the *Dialectics of Nature.* Like Engels, Teilhard believes that man is "a cosmic phenomenon."[84] But more than Marx and Engels, he deduces all the consequences by studying "total matter" along

---

* This expression was coined by Teilhard.
† *Plus-être* in the French. [TRANS.]

with "the whole phenomenon"—once again, not a metaphysical matter, but a material matter, the sensitive properties of which are rigorously examined with the most modern instruments of scientific analysis. This enables Teilhard to correct the numerous errors in the *Dialectics of Nature*. Engels' editor himself notes: "The history of the evolution of simple beings, sketched by Engels under the inspiration of Haeckel, no longer corresponds exactly with present knowledge." And so it goes with almost every chapter in the book.

It will have been noticed also that the theory of evolution leans constantly on facts, drawn from *practice,* from the experimentation of scientists.

But, one will object, what has become of the Marxist theory of the *class struggle?* In Teilhard's opinion, this is merely one aspect—peculiar to capitalism—of a much more general phenomenon: the process of socialization. I refer you to Volume V of the works of Teilhard, entitled *L'Avenir de l'Homme* (*The Future of Man*) and, in Volume III, to the article "Les Unités humaines naturelles" ("The Natural Human Unities"). As concerned with international life as Marx and Engels but more concerned than they with problems of *race* and *nation,* Teilhard shows us that conflicts between human groups—technico-professional groups or "classes," nations, races—are natural facts; moreover, that they are necessary steps in the process of socialization; that we are today, with the Cold War, with class, national and racial conflicts, in an age of extreme divergences; but that already a movement of pan-human convergence has been set in motion by the very tension and the power of our technical means—peaceful and military. From this movement, the planetary civilization will emerge, a symbiosis of all particular civilizations; and the scientist invites us, the underdeveloped peoples, to help construct the Civilization of the Universal. Marx and Engels did not know us. Teilhard restores our dignity and invites us to the *dialogue.* He writes: "Before the last upheavals that awakened the earth, peoples were only superficially alive; a world of energies was still asleep within each of them. Well, I imagine that these powers, still dormant within each natural human unity, in Europe, Asia, everywhere, are stirring and trying to come to light at this very moment; not to oppose and devour one another, but to rejoin and interfecundate one another. Fully conscious nations are needed for a total earth."[85] This is justification for our nationalism and our *Négritude,* all the more so because, according to the paleontologist, it was in Black Africa that *Homo sapiens* first appeared about 30,000 years ago.

Goal and Objectives

In Chapter I we saw how our compatriot, Berger, came to pose the problem of the ultimate goal of human action. In a recent article,[86] I tried to show that in his concept of prospective, Berger had been influenced by Teilhard de Chardin. Note the beginning of Teilhard's chapter on ultra-reflection in *Les Singularités de l'espèce humaine:* "Reflection induces foresight."[87] By the very fact that it is thought, comprehension of past and present, reflection—like an instrument of action—pushes us to study the future, the domain of action. That is what Teilhard's suggestion means. He continues: "I should like to explain how, by logically prolonging a certain law of recurrence, recognized as universally valid, one is led not to imagine the future of humanity, but at least to recognize the existence of certain conditions, certain contours, outside of which our world of tomorrow would be inconceivable . . . because it would contradict certain positive and definite characteristics of the world today."[88] Because of the progress of our knowledge, Teilhard and Berger are bolder than Marx and Engels concerning the problem of ends. But in their projection of the future, they respect the criteria of truth: theory and practice, coherence and fecundity—that is to say, efficacy.

The problem of the ends, of the ultimate goal of man's "generic activity," can thus find solution, for the scientist who follows the development of history, in the *retrospective-prospective* of evolution, according to the law of complexity-consciousness. According to this law, we have passed from apparently inanimate matter to the pre-life, thence to instinctive life, thence to reflective life, thence to co-reflective life. From this stage, which multiplies human relations by co-reflection and accelerates

the process of socialization, leading individuals and groups toward "pan-human convergence," we now progress toward the
ultra-reflective life, toward the *maximum-being*.

What constitutes this maximum-being? As we have said, for
Marx and Engels, it consists, negatively, in the elimination of
all material and spiritual alienations; positively, in the freedom
accorded individuals by the collective organization of society, to
develop fully in body and mind. To develop by labor, by ob-
jectivating themselves in nature thus transformed, and by ap-
propriating and integrating with nature. For Berger and even
more for Teilhard, this definition of the maximum-being, this
solution of the problem of the ends, is not false, but incomplete.
In Teilhard's opinion, if the objectives are *hic et nunc,* on earth
or in man, the same is not true of the ultimate *goal*. In the Teilhardian prospective, the growth of consciousness to ultra-reflection is related to complexification. It is made, not by a causal
push from behind, but by a final attraction from ahead. Not from
the "without" but from the "within."

Parenthetically, I should point out that Teilhard, without saying so, carries dialectical logic to its extreme consequences. It is
in line with this theory—and his practice as a scientist—that he
goes from cause to effect, from motive to end, from the "without"
to the "within" to find a coherent and effective solution for the
problem Marx and Engels posed. "In truth," writes Teilhard,
"for humanity to cohere, even in its present super-charged state,
a field of gravity that is both powerful and irreversible seems indispensable. This could not emanate collectively from a simple
cloud of reflective atoms but requires, as its source, a self-sustain-
ing and powerfully personalized star."[89] This deserves a comment; I shall return to it. Suffice it to say here that this personalized center that attracts all human centers in order to
develop them by organizing them, is the famous Omega point. It
is God. This is what emerges dialectically at the end of orthogenesis, from man's cosmic drift.

God, as Super-Person, is a problem that all civilizations, even
socialism, have posed, for it is a vital necessity. Jean Jaurès
poses it as follows:

Socialists today are forced by *the imperatives of the struggle* to stress materialism as absolute and total truth. After the victory, when they are able to examine it more closely, they will perceive that they cannot and must not abandon materialism, but rather complete it. They will realize that they are not expected to lose themselves in the supernatural, but that nature itself, opening its depths to the probing mind, lets God appear.[90]

In reality, what Marx and Engels criticize in the God of "revealed religions" is that He is posed "as a final principle by an outer impulse."[91] For Teilhard, it is precisely because the more "man consciously forges his own history, the less it is influenced by unforeseen effects," that he turns toward God, center of the maximum-being, that he turns to Him for an "inner necessity," as Engels would say. Significantly, Engels ended his introduction to *Dialectics of Nature* with a sentence that is already Teilhardian: "We have the certainty . . . that [if matter] will exterminate its highest creation, the thinking mind, it must somewhere else and at another time again produce it."[92]

Thus, in the middle of this twentieth century, we are pushed— or more exactly, drawn—toward that center of centers, that ultraconsciousness which is God. But, once again, this is merely the ultimate goal of our progress. Since Marx, since the decline of capitalism and the emergence of socialism, we have been at the threshold of the age of ultra-reflection, which will lead us from well-being to maximum-being before we are consummated in God. But first, we must build the earth, our earth. For the African, for the Senegalese, this need is all the more urgent because we have not yet even attained well-being. As one knows, our masses are still prey to disease, poverty, and ignorance.

Here the problem of the objectives of our action arises. Political objectives on the one hand, economic and social objectives on the other.

Analysis of our Negro-African *situation* will reveal that this was not the situation of Western Europe when Marx was writing *Capital*. In "Freedom, Independence, Development," a lecture delivered at the opening session of the Institute for Studies of Economic and Social Development, Gaston Berger made a penetrating analysis of our situation.

What was the situation of Western Europe during the second half of the nineteenth century? It was that of *independent nations,* politically the most powerful—the colonizing nations— with the greatest economic development. They shared the world and its wealth, thanks to their soldiers, their scientists, their technicians, their capital. The *socialist* revolution consisted less in a production of men, capital, and commodities, than in a transfer of capital-production and of commodity-distribution. It was a *family revolution,* as Marx and Engels proved, by demanding not the liberation of the colonized,* but that of the workers, of the metropolitan proletariat. Not until Lenin did Marxism become interested in the colonial problem, for reasons of political strategy.[93]

What is our African situation? What was it after the liberation of Europe? There were three independent nations in all: Ethiopia, Liberia, and South Africa. And in South Africa, Africans lived under oppression. The other territories suffered dependence, disease, poverty, and ignorance. The problem here, I have often repeated, was less a transfer of capital and goods than a production of men, capital, and goods; the problem here was not to eliminate classes by a class struggle within the nation; it was to bridge the gap between *developed* and *underdeveloped* nations. To take Senegal as an example, there was in fact no proletariat, since there was no bourgeoisie; there was no capital, no saving, therefore, no capitalists. There were only technico-professional groups whose interests, however divergent, were not opposed: government workers, small merchants, men in the liberal professions,† farmers, cattle-herders, fishermen, artisans. If capitalism existed, it was *foreign: Economic domination rested on political domination.* As in Europe—this was the one point in common— we had only to take over political power for the economic power to depend on the people. Such was our Negro-African situation, which imposed, to be sure, *different* political and economic objectives on us, different "intermediary aims," but especially, *different* means.

In a word, this *different* situation pointed out our own road to disalienation and transcendence: the Senegalese road to socialism,

* They referred only to European colonists.
† Like the high government officials, these were very few in number.

which is merely one version of the African road. Its first requirement was *political*. Accordingly, you will recall, I demanded, as
early as 1946, national *independence* and immediate internal
autonomy for all overseas territories.[94] As a matter of fact, this
was the primary condition for all other disalienations: economic,
social, cultural. Referring to political independence, Berger
observes:

> The bitterness of those who feel that they have thus been taken in,
> makes them sometimes unjust even toward freedom, considered as a
> formal right. And yet, it is this freedom which, first and foremost,
> renders everything possible. The absence of constraint does not suffice
> to enable one to enjoy true liberty; but it is nonetheless the indis-
> pensable first condition; it is the framework into which all the rest
> will be inserted. Without it, our works cease to belong to us. Liberty
> consecrates our dignity and makes us truly men.[95]

Previously, the Senegalese philosopher had distinguished between
liberty and independence.

> Liberty is a right; it is the absence of shackles, the possibility of acting
> as one wishes. A people is free when no other people can dictate its
> decisions. . . . Independence is quite another thing. It is a fact; it
> refers not to the friendly or hostile will of others, but to natural con-
> ditions which either exist or do not exist. Independence is the ability
> to be self-sufficient. To depend is to need others.[96]

The relevance of these definitions is proved by the word *freedom*
that our English-speaking neighbors use to translate *political
independence*.

We obtained this freedom from France in 1960. But we realized
that it was merely a juridical, nominal independence. And we
said so. We did even more, by trying to provide a content for this
empty frame that would make it a true independence. Upon
reflection, even juridical independence is not, of itself, political
independence. At any rate, not for the people. This poses, once
again, the problem of the *dictatorship of the proletariat*.

More exactly, it could not be posed for us Senegalese, since,
lacking a bourgeoisie, we Senegalese could have no proletariat.
As the Senegalese are a proletarian people by comparison with the

French, juridical independence, which restored our sovereignty, enabled us to solve the problem, on one condition: that Senegal should affirm—and practice—a policy not of neutralism but of nonalignment, while cooperating in friendship with the former colonizer. This we have done, and here again we encounter the *dialectics of theory and practice.* Moreover, the term *freedom-independence* expresses this dialectics. For us, the real problem was not one of dictatorship, but of democracy. Sovereignty, restored to the Senegalese people, had to be exercised *by this people and for this people.* This we have done in three steps: by suppressing the chiefdoms; by instituting a multi-party system; and by making the dominant party into a party of the masses.

This is more important than one may think. I believe that the positive contribution of the regimes called "socialist" is neither the one-party system nor the party of the cadres. The example set by these regimes is the best argument against them. That is where the shoe pinches. But let us go further. The *single party,* grouping intellectuals, workers and peasants, was conceivable in Europe after the socialist revolution, to liquidate the vestiges of capitalism. In an underdeveloped country, where independence has been the work of all, as a national revolution, the single party seemed to present the danger of government by clique, the danger of sclerosis. In Europe, it is accompanied by bureaucracy. As it becomes a party of cadres to which one gains admission only after long apprenticeship, it ceases to be "a party of the masses." The formula of the *dominant party* seemed best to us. It rejects violence, which is useless here. It appeals to nationalist sentiment—to the head and to the heart, not to fear. This is why the dominant party is the party of the masses: a political organization of the nation evolving toward the nation's construction by *socialization*—in other words, by planning, conceived as integral development, with the nation and each individual citizen progressing from underdevelopment to development.

Before leaving the objectives, I should like to discuss a *general intermediate aim* that European socialists neglect. Though it is true that the *ultimate goal* of man's generic activity is his realization as a god through love, we must find this love here and now, as we attain the political, economic, social, and cultural

objectives. Both Berger and Teilhard have emphasized this point
too much for us to pass over it in silence. European Marxists
speak negatively about struggle, and positively about science,
production, normative ethics, sometimes about art—and never
about love. Nevertheless, if they have eliminated the love of God,
they have not long been able to curb the love of men, which
today once again wells up even in Russian poetry. As if "socialist
realism" could ignore this human reality which Europe had
deified. Referring to space research, Berger sees it as proof that
"men today are becoming gradually conscious of their *raison
d'être,* which is to seek out one another, to meet one another,
and to unite."[97]

But it is Teilhard who proposes the most coherent theory
concerning the *nature and role of love in socialization,* founded,
as always, on the facts of experience.[98] Starting from the law of
complexification-consciousness, he shows us that progress in life
is linked to "centrity": to the union, center to center, of corpuscles
and beings. For centers contain the maximum of psyche or spiritual energy. His second observation is that "true union (or synthesis) does not confuse; it differentiates"[99] by personalizing each
component. . . . What would be the use of human activity—
political, economic, social, cultural revolutions—what would be
the use of well-being if it did not lead to that maximum-being
that we feel in Love-Union? Love for one's mate, one's family,
one's fatherland, on the planet Earth? Even politicians, to win the
people's support in the midst of tension and international conflict, claim that peace is the goal of war. And they are not entirely
wrong, since these tensions and conflicts only express the painful
parturition of a new world of brotherhood, of *love.* Teilhard's
socialization, our socialism is nothing but the *technical and
spiritual organization of human society by the intelligence and
the heart.* After satisfying their animal needs and acquiring well-
being by democracy and planning, men will then be able, in
union, which is love, to realize their maximum-being. It is this
Love-Union that we find as the focal center of art, ethics, and
religion.

To explain, let us once again be guided by Teilhard. In the
article *Human Energy* that provides the title for Volume VI of

his works, he affirms that love is the "higher form of human energy." Placing himself, like Marx and Engels, in the movement of history, he shows that "universal love really presents itself to our experience as the superior phase of a transformation already begun in the mass of the Nous-sphere," as a general objective and final goal. Considered in this movement: (1) Man totalizes his individual acts solely by love. Most often, he puts only a part of himself in his action. But if he considers the goal—human convergence with God—then, "with the universe, in the least of his acts, he can establish total contact over the entire surface and in the depths of his being." (2) By totalizing our individual acts, love totalizes us at the same time—I mean that it personalizes us. This personalization, the synthesis of our faculties (intelligence and heart) and of our activities (thought and action) is also their symbiosis, for let us not forget that *union differentiates*. So it is that love for woman not only exalts each of man's faculties, but also makes of him a superior man, whether he be scientist, technician, or artist. "If human love is so powerful," Teilhard asks, "how much greater the vibration when our beings encounter Omega?" (3) Men are totalized, and socialized, in humanity solely by love. "The passage from the individual to the collective is the crucial problem of human energy," says Teilhard.[100]

Although all the present political regimes—democracy, socialism, Communism—have as their goal totalization and socialization without depersonalization, they fail in their attempt. This is because they sacrifice the part to the whole, the person to the collectivity. Since a materialist postulate underlies this, and since the collectivity is conceived solely as a technical organization, it does not attract; to push the individuals toward it, one must resort to constraint and violence. This is the reason for the failures. But if one conceives of the collectivity as human convergence cemented by liberty, equality, fraternity—terms that Marx scorned—and if one places love of the Super-Person above human love, there will naturally be a powerful attraction to group individuals without constraint. For, once again, "union differentiates," love personalizes.

I have often spoken of the role of underdeveloped nations in the building of the international community. Because the Negro

Africans have kept a sense of brotherhood and dialogue, because they are inspired by religions that preach love and, above all, because they live those religions, they can propose positive solutions for the construction of the international as well as the national community. The importance of love as essential energy, the stuff of life, is at the heart of *Négritude,* underlying the black man's ontology. Everywhere the couple—male-female—translates the integrality of the being. To be sure, procreation as the means of perpetuating the family and species occupies an important place in Negro-African society. But let us not be deceived: Beyond the embrace of the bodies is the complementary union of souls. "Thus," Marcel Griaule writes, "every human being, from the beginning, was provided with two souls of different sex, or rather with two principles corresponding to two distinct persons inside of each individual."[101] In Negro-African mythology, the combination *Word-and-Music* stands at the origin of creation. By uttering this formula, God created all beings, for it is at the same time feeling, thought, and action. This creative energy is love. It is composed of two complementary elements: music, "the oil, symbol of masculinity, added to the feminine flow of speech."[102]

Method and Means

I shall have nothing to add about the method of dialectical logic, which has already been discussed in line with Marx, Engels, and Hegel. The failures or at least the limitations of so-called "socialist" regimes stem precisely from the fact that they are not always faithful to this method.[103] The problem is whether the two socialist theoreticians were right to reverse Hegelian dialectics, whether dialectics already exists in nature or whether it is only "reflected" in the mind. The problem is that of materialism rather than of dialectics.

In *Materialism and Empirio-Criticism,* Lenin maintains that the word "matter" merely designates "objective reality, which is given to man by his sensations and which is copied, photographed, and reflected by our sensations, while existing independently of them."[104] This brutal, categorical definition Merleau-Ponty views simply as a kind of general warning, for he cannot forget the

Notebooks on Hegel in which Lenin's thought is so delicately shaded. Furthermore, Engels himself recovers slightly from his naturalism:

> Natural science, like philosophy, has hitherto entirely neglected the influence of men's activity on their thought; both know only nature on the one hand and thought on the other. But it is precisely the *alteration of nature by man,* not solely nature as such, which is the most essential and immediate basis of human thought, and it is in the measure that man has learned to change nature that his intelligence has increased.[105]

At the beginning of his chapter on Lenin's philosophy, Lefebvre admits: "The discoveries that led directly to present-day nuclear physics (electronic particles, etc.) were accomplished without the Marxists, outside of their research and analyses. However, these discoveries upset the old concepts of matter. Going further, he recognizes in the presentations of Marx and Engels a "gap" that Lenin hoped to fill. Lefebvre even admits that Engels' "texts" do not satisfactorily meet the new problems. New problems posed by the new scientific discoveries and non-Marxian philosophy. New problems that Lenin proposed to solve. "Unfortunately," Lefebvre observes, "Lenin no more than Marx or Engels provided the authoritative treatment of certain crucial philosophical problems that we might have hoped for."[106] We do not propose to deny Lenin's genius nor his decisive contribution to the thorough study of Marxism. He it was who most vigorously insisted that Marxism is neither economism nor historicism nor sociologism nor relativism. But when he maintains that "the sole 'property' of matter is . . . the property of being objective reality, of existing outside of our cognition,"[107] he reverts to Engels. By assimilating matter to being, no more no less, he is not meeting the new scientific problems: He is dealing in metaphysics, if not dodging the problem.

Does dialectical logic "prevail throughout nature"[108] before being reflected in the mind? Is "dialectical thought" merely a "copy" of the historical motion of nature? This is the first question to answer. The proposition of Engels and Lenin contains a contradiction in principle: It ends up by inserting in matter its opposite, which is mind, by placing the subject in the object. As Merleau-Ponty says, this is a return to "naive realism," rendering knowledge of the truth impossible:

> In fact, from the moment when consciousness and being are placed face to face like two external realities, when consciousness, as a simple reflection, is struck with a radical doubt . . . consciousness no longer disposes of any criterion for distinguishing between knowledge and ideology.[109]

Here, as elsewhere, to answer the question it suffices to return, not to *Capital,* but to Marx's philosophical works, especially to the "Eleven Theses on Feuerbach." "The chief defect of all materialism up to now . . . is, that the object, reality, what we apprehend through our senses, is understood only in the form of the *object* or *contemplation*; but not as *sensuous human activity,* as *practice.*" Thus in his view, the activity of the mind—thought— must be considered "as *objective* activity."[110] Obviously, one can criticize Marx for calling "objective" and "material" the activity of the subject: "thought" as well as "speech." It remains true nonetheless that the "First Thesis on Feuerbach" is confirmed by modern physics. In the act of knowledge, in the search for the truth of the *being,* the scientist or subject acts on the object: He alters it by observing it. As Pierre Guaydier writes in reference to Heisenberg's "relations of uncertainty," "the scientist who performs an experiment acts, more or less, on the phenomena to be measured, modifies them by his intervention and consequently falsifies the results."[111] It is essentially in the confrontation of subject and object—and vice versa—that one finds dialectical logic, the act of knowledge, which is at once theory and practice. By *theory* I mean the "categories" of understanding, and, by *practice,* the methods and techniques of the subject. "The qualities of the scientific real," Gaston Bachelard concludes, "are thus, primarily, the functions of our rational methods. To constitute a scientific fact, it is necessary to apply a coherent technique."[112] Scientists go so far as to suspect that the most minute particles of matter—photons, protons, and electrons—have no reality outside of our thinking.[113] It follows that dialectics and consequently knowledge is essentially an *élan* of the mind. "Comprehension,"

Bachelard writes, "has a dynamic axis; it is a spiritual drive, an *élan vital*."[114] How far we now are from the "reflection," from the "copy"! This is a dialectical turn that almost rehabilitates Hegel.

But for the moment, let's not go that far. If we limit ourselves to the first thesis on Feuerbach, we note a resemblance with *Negro-African gnosiology*. According to the theory of the "reflection" and the classical theory, the act of knowledge is the work of the *reasoning-eye;* for the Negro African, it is the work of the *reasoning-embrace*. Knowledge, truth, is born of transcendence, from the active union of subject and object. More than a synthesis, it is a symbiosis, the daughter of *Love*. But it is more intuition than analysis, more induction than deduction. Is it not significant that Bachelard, the philosopher of the sciences, has rehabilitated induction and intuition? An intuition verified and confirmed, to be sure, by discursive mathematical analysis.

The first question leads to a second: Which is the primitive, "basic" element, mind or matter? Marx and Engels reply that it is matter. Teilhard de Chardin attacks this thesis in the first part of the *Phenomenon of Man*. Obviously, to answer the question pertinently, matter must be given not a metaphysical, but a physical definition that is both coherent and effective. It is necessary to analyze matter in such a way as to enumerate its attributes or qualities along with its simplest elements. For "in reality, there are no simple phenomena; the phenomenon is a network of relations. There is no *simple* nature; substance is a texture of attributes."[115]

Teilhard begins by analyzing "elemental matter," that is to say, taken "at any point and in any given volume." He recognizes three attributes: plurality, unity, energy. He sees "total matter" or matter "considered in its physical and concrete reality" as "a system by its plurality, a totum by its unity, a quantum by its energy." But, since evolutionism, Teilhard observes, "the positive knowledge of things is identified with the study of their development." Thus, in the new perspective of space-time, matter "appears as a mass in process of transformation." In this development we can best grasp its true nature. A first law of matter, arrived at by experimental analysis, is that all bodies are composed of atoms, of a nucleus and one or several electrons. The second law that we know is that all bodies derive from the atom by arrangement, by *complexification*. The third law is that of energy, which rests on two principles: 1) The conservation of energy: No new energy is born of a synthesis; what is gained on one side is lost on the other. 2) The dissipation of energy: Every synthesis utilizes a fraction of energy "which is lost in the form of heat." The result is that the more organized the world becomes, "the more the energy-quantum of the world comes into play, the more it is consumed."[116] So much for the "without" of matter.

At this point in his reasoning, Teilhard de Chardin invites us to examine the "within." To start with, he recalls "the quarrel between materialists and the upholders of a spiritual interpretation, between finalists and determinists." As a working hypothesis, he proposes "each sees only half the problem." For each sees only one side of the phenomenon. Yet matter has its "within," which "appears in definite qualitative or quantitative connections with the developments that science recognizes in cosmic energy"[117]: in the "without."

In contemporary physics, we perceive in the material unity of nature different "spheres," "thresholds," or "levels," "each characterized by the dominance of certain factors which become imperceptible or negligible in the neighboring sphere or level."[118] Thus, in the realm of physico-chemistry, objects seem governed solely by their outward determinisms. But as we go up the scale of life—bacteria, plants, insects, vertebrates—we can no longer keep the same intellectual attitude. And determinism breaks down completely with man, whose "within"—thought—we can grasp directly. Consequently, to reason in a coherent manner, this "within," this thought, exists everywhere, under pressure, in matter, even if only in a rudimentary form of pre-life. Because life cannot be born of "spontaneous generation," as Marx believed.

At this point, the materialists and the upholders of a spiritual interpretation will object: "If everything in nature is basically alive or, at least, in a pre-vital state, how is it possible for a mechanistic science of matter to be built up and to triumph?" Teilhard de Chardin answers this question by indicating how thought "suddenly appears and then as suddenly bursts through into certain other regions of our experience." For this purpose, he makes three observations: 1) The "within" of things in the pre-vital state assumes the same granulation as matter. It is atomic. 2) At this stage, "the constituents of consciousness . . . complicate and differentiate their kind, little by little, with the passage of duration." 3) The development of thought into consciousness is directly proportionate to the organization, to the complexification of matter. "Spiritual perfection (our conscious 'centrity') and material synthesis (or complexity) are but the two aspects or connected parts of a single phenomenon."[119]

And so the question posed finds its answer. In the pre-life, the centers of consciousness, because they are numerous, unorganized, and rather homogeneous, are subjected to determinism, to mathematical laws. In life, on the contrary, because they are "less numerous and at the same time more highly individualized,"[120] they appear to us in their spontaneity, in their freedom. The contradiction begins to be resolved. It will be completely resolved by Teilhard's dialectical *revolution*.

This is presented in *The Phenomenon of Man* and in an article of Volume II, "Les Singularités de l'espèce humaine." A first fact imposes itself, he observes: In our daily activity, we feel ourselves both dependent on and independent of matter. "To think, we must eat. But what a variety of thoughts we get out of one slice of bread!"[121] In other words, there is no "mechanical equivalent" in matter for thought, although the two phenomena are related. To avoid the old dualism of the philosophers and scientists, which Marx and Engels did not terminate, and carrying dialectical logic to its ultimate consequences, Teilhard holds that there are not two realities but a single one under the appearance of two phenomena: not mind and matter, but rather mind-matter, just as there is space-time. Underlying the "without" and the "within" there is only a single energy, which appears in two aspects. The one, tangential energy, is that of the physicists and chemists. It links the particles materially one to the other. The second, radial energy, psychically links the centers of consciousness one to the other. This is the energy we must consider as "the elemental stuff of the universe." "Upsetting end over end the classical perspective," Teilhard decides "that of the two, radial energy is primitive and consistent, tangential energy being merely the subproduct statistically engendered by the inter-reactions of elementary 'centers' of consciousness, imperceptible in the pre-life but clearly perceptible in our experience from a sufficiently advanced degree of an arrangement of matter."[122] This dialectical turn presents a double advantage of coherence and fecundity. On the one hand, the physico-chemical laws remain valid in the pre-life. On the other hand, consciousness escapes from those laws to establish itself in liberty. This is not all; Beyond material well-being, spiritual maximum-being—the flowering of the soul, of the intelligence and of the heart—is confirmed as the ultimate goal of human activity.

As already noted, this new dialectics does not so much contradict Marx's thought as deepen and complete it by removing any trace of one-sidedness. This one-sidedness is precisely the weak point of the so-called "socialist" regimes, of the Communist regimes. "Lenin's gnosiology," Merleau-Ponty remarks, "merging dialectics with materialist metaphysics, preserves dialectics, but embalmed, outside of us, in an exterior reality."[123] This unilateral reality is the party of the cadres, as we have seen. Between the dialectical revolution of the "within" and the "without," between permanent transcendence and the State—which is the apparatus for the preservation of the party and the suppression of all spontaneity—they have chosen the State. Outside of the party and the State, there is no knowledge, no truth. This is not even faithful to Lenin's teachings, as we shall soon see.

To repeat, it is in relation to the goal and objectives of human activity that the means of realization are sought and defined, as a function of well-being and maximum-being. Technical means, in the broad sense of the term, are resumed in planning, and political means are decided by the party. Once again, we find only general indications concerning these means in Marx and Engels. We must wait for Lenin before we get more detailed, lucid, and fruitful explanations. This is why I said a moment ago that the present dogmatism of the Communist party is not in line with Lenin's teachings. It is true that, since the death of Stalin, Khrushchev has labored to rehabilitate Lenin's thinking.

I shall add nothing about the political means. These were discussed earlier, when we examined the problem of the dictatorship of the proletariat. At that time, I opposed the Marxist-Leninist thesis to our thesis of democratic pluralism with a dominant party.

But I must return to the problem of planning, though I shall not discuss it at length. I should like, nevertheless, to examine with you the four conditions of Marx and Engels.

1. You know the UPS position on the nationalization of the means of production: It is realistic. As I recently wrote:

Nationalization is not an end in itself. It is a means, among others, to realize the socialist objective: the development of production and the equitable distribution of the products.

To nationalize, one must have private national capital and an adequate supply of national technicians. This is not the case with us. Since the goal is *socialization,* we shall reach it more surely by engaging in a dialogue with foreign capitalists. It is a question of associating with them under certain well-defined conditions. To be exact, it is a question, of retaining the *direction* of affairs, of guaranteeing them a fair share of the profits in return for their services. The essential condition is that the accord enable the nation to develop its productivity and, therefore, its wealth. In an underdeveloped country, the Revolution—I mean economic independence—can only be carried out step by step. This is the meaning of our Investment Code, which favors capital invested in the framework of the Plan.[124]

On second thought, nationalization, at bottom, is merely another organism for development.* As you know, even before voting the first Four-Year Plan, the Senegalese Government had created various organisms for development: administrative—regions, *cercles,* districts; economic—Office of Agricultural Commercialization, Regional Centers of Technical Assistance for Development, Centers of Rural Expansion; and financial—Crédit du Sénégal, Senegalese Development Bank, Senegalese Bank of Commerce and Industry. The main thing is to reach the goal, which is the *maximum-being,* and more immediately, the objectives of *well-being.* Nationalization is merely one means among

* *Structure d'accueil* in the French. [TRANS.]

others, the effectiveness of which is measured by the realities of the national situation.

2. The second condition of good planning is scientific research —for Engels' reasons, advanced earlier, and especially because planning is the organization of a more human future. One can do this only by developing research, which will embrace all the sciences: not merely the so-called "exact" or "fundamental" sciences—mathematics, physics, chemistry—but also the natural sciences—climatology, soil science, botany, zoology; especially the human sciences—geography, history, anthropology, sociology. The planner must control all his knowledge, all the *facts of evolving nature,* in order to prepare the human future.

This "science of the Future," founded on the totality of sciences and the most modern techniques, is called Prospective. It is our good fortune that prospective was created by a Senegalese from St. Louis, Gaston Berger. Starting from the Blondelian theory of knowledge which is "thought oriented toward action,"[125] our compatriot solidly established Prospective on the notion of operative time, as distinguished from existential time. The latter is the time of the poets and is spent in "wailing and regret" and anxiety. Operative time is the time of action. It imposes order on our projects. . . .

As a science of the future, Prospective leans on this time of labor. But our notion of the future is itself modified by that of operative time, conceived as time of creation. "The future," writes Berger, "is no longer that which must inevitably happen. . . . It is what the world as a whole is going to do."[126] You can recognize the Teilhardian accent in that sentence. It is not there by accident.

Prospective, as meditation on time, is founded on four principles: (1) It is less a science than a method—it is an attitude; a "change of focus." Prospective reflection makes us seize the future as it will be, with its complexity, mobility, risks, and surprises. (2) The glance, to be effective, must carry "afar," distinguishing the remote from the near future. To take a timely example, we are being prospective when we see the Malians as our friends of tomorrow. (3) Beyond the economic facts, prospective sticks to human facts. (4) Placing man at the heart of our problems—man often as means, but always as end—the prospective searcher is compelled to pose clearly the problem of the ends.[127]

All that is familiar to the Senegalese. A truly strange coincidence is this encounter between Berger's thinking and our Senegalese problems. We have been practicing prospective without realizing it. No doubt because, like Berger, we are Senegalese.

3. The third condition for good planning is naturally the preparation of an economic and social development plan. To be effective, this plan must meet certain requirements.

First, to organize a more human future, it must be prospective. It must be based on the situation in Senegal, on a scientific inventory of our economic and social data. In other words, to prepare the future, it must use knowledge of our past and our present, thanks to scientific research. This requirement was met by the 2,000-page inventory prepared under the direction of Father Lebret from October, 1958, to July, 1959.

Secondly, the plan must select precise objectives of economic growth and social development. In economic growth, the important point is to establish a harmonious balance between the various sectors of the economy: infrastructure, industry, rural economy. This balance must even be found within each sector— between heavy industry and processing industry, between agriculture and stock-raising or fishing—but previously it will exist between the economic infrastructure and the administrative infrastructure.

Here as elsewhere, we have rejected prefabricated models. We have not allowed ourselves to be seduced by Russian, Chinese, or Scandinavian models. After an objective examination, we have learned lessons from the successes and failures of the different "socialist experiments." Above all, we have observed that formulas like "priority for heavy industry" or "agrarian reform" have no magic power within themselves; applied dogmatically, they have produced partial failures. That is why we established priorities as follows: "infrastructure, rural economy, processing industry, heavy industry," in line with reasonable requirements and our realities. To transform, one must first produce something to transform; before producing machine tools, we must produce living men—that is to say, we must have consumer goods. The distribution of land to the peasants does not get them very far unless they have previously been given the means to make that land fertile: modern knowledge and modern instruments. Lenin, who was more realistic than Marx, more favorable to compromise than is generally supposed, had begun to perceive these truths, from contact with Russian realities. He had conceived the New Political Economy as "a strategic withdrawal from earlier objectives,[128] as "a fruitful compromise," in the sense indicated in his *Left-wing Communism: An Infantile Disorder.* Once again, for us as for Lenin, it is a question of rejecting prefabricated models. In this connection, François Perroux observes, "If the patterns of growth prepared by Westerners were accepted—even along the most general lines—by the underdeveloped countries, they would cause the latter disasters and servitude."[129]

By social development, I mean the development of hygiene and health, of municipal administration and housing, of education and culture. It is the production of man by the fight against disease and ignorance. This is the major objective of the Plan, more important than economic growth. For it, the Senegalese Government has earmarked 34.7 per cent of public investments and 20.5 per cent of total investments.

For the objectives of economic growth and social development, a good plan must fix and find means of realization: financial means and cultural means. I shall not dwell on the financial means. In the twentieth century, when aid to underdeveloped countries is the fashion—for reasons of human solidarity and also for political strategy—it is relatively easy to locate capital. Senegal finds it without great difficulty.

As for the cultural means, contemporary economists have given these an importance they did not enjoy in Marxian economics, though Marx stressed the role of consciousness and will in the transformation of the world. Perroux writes: "Development is the combination of a people's mental and social changes, which makes it apt to increase its real global output cumulatively and durably."[130] The problem, therefore, especially in an underdeveloped country, is to awaken "dormant energies," to combat prejudices, routine, inferiority complexes, and the fatalistic spirit. In a word, we must awaken the national conscience to the call of *Négritude*.

Understanding this, the Senegalese Government decided to awaken the consciousness of the masses. We hope to do this by Community Development,* a major means of realizing the Plan —to be sure, in the Community Development Centers and in all the developmental organisms—not to mention instruction, which becomes education by the reform of textbooks and teaching methods. Briefly, it is a matter of inspiring each Senegalese, especially the cadres, to exercise initiative and creativeness.

But the Government cannot and must not do it all. It must be guided and helped by the party. This means that we must rethink the role of the party, the role of the UPS, in the light of our Senegalese realities. Our party must be the consciousness of the masses. Its role is twofold. In the first place, it must be the echo of the popular aspirations—not only their echo, but their scientific expression as well. As Lenin wrote: "We can exercise power only on condition that we express exactly what the people are conscious of."[131] But the party must do more: It must guide the masses. The consciousness of the masses, who lack education and culture, still remains confused, lost in the fog of animal needs. It does not rise to the level of "political consciousness, a superior form of consciousness."[132] This can only reach the masses from the outside, from the intellectuals. Again, it was Lenin who wrote: "Socialist doctrine was born of philosophical, historical and economic theories, drawn up by the educated representatives of the privileged classes, by the intellectuals. The founders of modern scientific socialism were themselves, by virtue of their social position, bourgeois intellectuals."[133] This is a far cry from leftist verbalism.

Better still, the party must combat bureaucracy even more vigorously than technocracy. The technocrats believe that all problems must be considered—and resolved—in the perspective of science and technique alone, and they forget that the conscious will of men is a *sine qua non* of the revolution. The bureaucrats forget that the efficiency of labor is measured neither by the

* *Animation* in the French. [TRANS.]

amount of paper blackened nor even by membership in the government party, but by technical knowledge and rational working methods. The conquest of power is one thing: The peaceful organization of the revolution is something quite different. This is what Lenin means when he writes:

> Our point of view has changed radically. Formerly, we placed the center of gravity on the political struggle, the revolution, the conquest of power. Today, the center of gravity has moved. It bears on the peaceful labor of cultural organization. To begin, it would be enough for us to have a real bourgeois culture, to be able to get along without types characterized by prebourgeois cultures, that is to say, by bureaucratic or feudal culture.[134]

All of which should stimulate us to reconsider the role of the UPS.

4. The final condition of good planning is the transformation of social structures. As we have seen, a plan is prepared—and implemented—not only for man but by man. This means that man must be urged to work, above all, to innovate and create. Man in general, and especially the most disinherited groups—laborers, peasants, shepherds, fishermen, artisans. This the Senegalese Government has understood. Accordingly, we have frozen the government workers' salaries and discontinued indemnities for ministers and deputies. This is the justification for our Labor Code and social legislation, one of the most progressive in Africa. This also explains a whole series of concrete measures taken on behalf of our artisans, especially on behalf of the rural population, such as the organization of cooperatives.

Because it has met these four conditions, the Senegalese Plan should prove to be a most effective instrument of development.

I shall not conclude without examining the spiritual means proposed by Marx and Engels and completed by Lenin. For the socialist thinkers, modern morality appropriate for the contemporary situation excludes religion, especially revealed religions such as Christianity and Islam. In my opinion, the weakest part of Lefebvre's book on Marxism is his treatment of Marxian morality. Attacking religion as traditional morality, Lefebvre writes:

Like ethics, law has always sanctioned existing relations and conditions, so as to immobilize them and bend them toward domination by the economically privileged and political ruling classes. Moral
alienation is therefore not separated, historically, socially, practically,
from other forms of alienation: general ideology, law, religion, etc.[135]

I take issue with this statement, placing myself, to start with, on
Marx's own terrain, on the dual level of the theoretical and
practical—I mean the historical.

As indicated in the first part of this discussion, law and state,
religion and ethics have their historical truth. These ideologies
enable man to transcend the third stage of production and the
second alienation. According to Marx himself, as spiritual products of the rising class, they aim to fill the void made by turning
man's products against man. They tend toward the appropriation
of these products by the individuals, toward the reunification of
subject and object, of nature divided against herself. It is true
that the "rising class," on becoming the "dominant class," hastens
to transform these ideologies into instruments of domination.
Nevertheless, these ideologies remain valid. It suffices to rethink
them by bringing them up-to-date, to restore their spiritual
effectiveness. This is the meaning of religious reform. Marx recognized this, when he praised Luther for having "annulled *external*
religiosity while making religiosity the *inner* essence of man."[136]
Let us call attention to a contradiction. Marx condemns traditional law—the state, religion, ethics, and family—only to oppose
them by a modern law—morality, family, and art at the service
of the masses. Logic (and dialectics) would make him proceed
to recommend a modern State and religion as well. This is precisely what we must do, and are doing, in Senegal. Here I shall
limit my remarks to religion, considered as the totality of spiritual
values, as the source of an effective morality. I shall confine myself to Christianity and Islam, following the historical and the
alphabetical order. Two preliminary observations are in order.

The first is that Christianity and Islam, though revealed religions, nonetheless base their ethics on objective reality. Their
moral codes are natural, like Marx's. As Claude Tresmontant
writes, "We both accept the same Master, the Real, and the same
method of analysis: the rational, scientific method." Secondly,

Christians and Moslems readily admit that in practice most of
their co-religionists betray the principles of their respective moral
codes, that they are not practicing. Tresmontant states, "one must
distinguish carefully between Christian ethics and the mores that
all too often throughout history Christians have exhibited to the
world."[137] But does one not read, even in *Pravda,* violent criticisms of the deviations, negligence, or dishonesty of numerous
leaders and bureaucrats?

After those preliminary observations, I now return to Lefebvre's
statements, which unfortunately are for once too categorical. For
it is simply not true that Christian and Islamic ethics have
"always sanctioned existing relations and conditions, so as to
immobilize and bend them toward domination by the economically privileged and political ruling classes." Christianity and
Islam from the beginning have favored scientific research and
combated the prevailing moral order. Throughout their history
they have periodically reacted against the inevitable crystallizations of their respective ethics.

First, Christianity. Jesus was a revolutionary. In his sermons, he
protested against Roman ethics—that of the colonizers—and
against the ancient law of Israel. Born poor, he took a sympathetic interest in the fate of the poor and oppressed of all races
and religions. He repeats the words of the prophet Isaiah: "The
Spirit of the Lord is upon me, because he hath anointed me to
preach the gospel to the poor; he hath sent me to heal the
broken-hearted, to preach deliverance to the captives, and re-
covering of sight to the blind, to set at liberty them that are
bruised."[138]

As for Mohammed, who appears on the scene to confirm the
teaching of the Bible and Jesus, he writes: "And serve Allah.
Ascribe no thing as partner unto Him. Show kindness unto
parents, and unto near kindred, and orphans, and the needy,
and unto the neighbour who is of kin unto you and the neighbour who is not of kin, and the fellow-traveller and the wayfarer
and the slaves whom your right hands possess."[139] Mohammed
comes not only to confirm but also to complete. That is why the
Koran carefully regulates the spiritual and social organization of
society. Born an Arab, Mohammed proposes first to perfect the

Arab community by making it overcome its anarchy and tribalism. Above and beyond that, he aims, like Jesus, at all men. He labors for the establishment of a new society, for the birth of a new man. Thus Mohammed reveals himself as a liberator of women, contrary to what the average European believes. Like Christianity, Islam introduces universal values into human society.

> In fact, the socialism of Islam conforms to human nature. It satisfies the dignity and interests of all the citizens. To the worker, it guarantees a decent living standard and a sure future; to the man with capital to invest, it opens vast horizons in production under state control; finally, it is applied to all citizens without distinction and could not become the appanage of the faithful of one religion to the exclusion of those of another.[140]

Mustapha al-Siba'f belongs to the most recent group of Islamic reformers, the School of Arab Socialism, which takes its inspiration from the Koran, the Sunna and traditions, interpreting them in the light of contemporary realities. This gives me an opportunity once again to recommend the magazine *Orient* (published in Paris), one of the organs of these reformers.

Mustapha al-Siba'f's article should be compared to the social encyclicals of recent popes, especially Pope John's *Mater et Magistra*. The encyclicals react against the deviations of historical Christianity and take issue with a morality that preferred to concentrate on individual sin. With ever increasing vigor, they stress "the crimes committed collectively, nation against nation, race against race, social class against social class."[141] As for Islam, this is but a continuation of a long struggle against scleroses that affect every ideology, every social organism. In fact, immediately after the death of Jesus, first the Apostles, then Saint Paul, and later the Church Fathers took pains to complete Christ's teaching by spelling out the rules of Christian ethics as it confronts new situations. I am thinking particularly of Saint Basil and Saint Gregory the Great, who forcefully insisted that the right of property has limits and that excessive wealth is "for the common usage of all."[142]

Furthermore, socialism—Marxism in particular—is a reaction

of Christian origin against a bourgeois evolution of historical Christianity. Several of its ideas—such as the concept of *aliena-tion*—have their roots in Christian theology. This is hardly surprising, for it is false to claim with the Marxists that Christianity and Islam scorned, or even neglected, the sciences.

In his lecture "Un Musulman devant le monde chrétien" ("A Moslem Facing the Christian World"), the former Moroccan Ambassador to the Federal Republic of Germany, Abdelkébir El Fassi, advocates cooperation between the two religions: "Far from being an obstacle on the road to material progress, Islam compels its followers to keep constantly in the vanguard of earthly progress."[143] And he quotes these verses from the Koran: "Tell them, O Mohammed, that those who know are worth infinitely more than those who do not know." "Seek knowledge from the cradle to the grave." "Seek knowledge, even as far as China, if need be." As a matter of fact, the West owed the transmission of Greek sciences to the Arabs. Let us demolish a bulwark of prejudice by pointing this out: The Arab invasion that Charles Martel stopped at Poitiers was not an invasion of barbarians; on the contrary, the Arabs were bringing Western Europe a sum of knowledge and techniques that was to benefit Spain in particular.[144]

As for Christianity, Werner Jaeger shows in *Early Christianity and the Greek Paideia*[145] that the Apostles and their successors had soon felt the need for the most advanced culture of that time: Greek culture. That was the *sine qua non* for the effective propagation of Christianity. Abandoning Hebrew and Aramaic, St. John wrote his gospel in Greek. But it was after the invasion of Western Europe by German barbarians that Christianity became the guardian of the sciences and techniques of Greco-Roman civilization. One owes to it in the West, as to Islam in the East, the founding of the first universities. Scholasticism in the Middle Ages, developed in these universities, was more than a recipe of forms; it was in truth a method of open discussion, of research, as Joseph Pieper recently indicated in *La Table Ronde*. Subsequently, scholasticism, with "the Greek concept of the Cosmos," collapsed, yielding "to a mathematical philosophy of Christian inspiration."[146]

The task for us Senegalese is therefore clear. To build our socialism by implementing our Plan, we must not neglect the spiritual means contained in those religions. We must return to the roots to restore their meaning to these religions, that is to say, their interiority, which Feuerbach, without perhaps measuring the full implications of his statement, called "the immediate liaison of the individual with the universal." For that is what "religion" is: a liaison by reciprocal integration of subject and object, of man and universe. Let us simply be careful to remember that man is "the whole man and all men."

In the struggle of the blocs, the conflict of ideologies, the profusion of scientific discoveries and technical inventions, we must keep a cool head and an attentive heart. It is not a question of rejecting all these ideologies, discoveries, and inventions. It is rather a question of not accepting them without examination. Once again, we must assimilate, not be assimilated.* More exactly, it is a question of remaining deeply rooted in our *Négritude*, of integrating it with the most modern, fruitful, and effective discoveries and inventions. This is what we have been doing for several years, by integrating socialism with *Négritude*.

* This is a restatement of a famous comment Senghor first made in 1945. [Trans.]

Notes

Nationhood

1. Ahmed Ben Salah, in *Esprit*, 1957.
2. Denis de Rougemont, "Fédéralisme et Nationalisme," *Fédération*, September–October, 1954.
3. Henri Lefebvre, "Le Marxisme et la pensée française," and Lucien Goldmann, "Propos Dialectiques," in *Les Temps modernes*, No. 137–38 (July–August, 1957).
4. Pierre Bigo, *Marxisme et Humanisme* (Paris: Presses Universitaires de France, 1953), and Léopold Sédar Senghor, "Marxisme et Humanisme," *La Revue socialiste*, March, 1948.
5. Karl Marx, *Capital:* Vol. I: *Process of Capitalistic Production* (Chicago: Charles H. Kerr & Co., 1906), p. 42.
6. *Ibid.*, p. 46.
7. Karl Marx, "Alienated Labour," in *Karl Marx: Early Writings*, trans. and ed. T. B. Bottomore (London: C. A. Watts & Co., 1963), 1st manuscript, p. 128.
8. *Ibid.*, p. 122.
9. *Ibid.*, p. 126.
10. See André Vène, *Vie et doctrine de Karl Marx* (Paris: Editions de la Nouvelle France, 1946), p. 315.
11. *Capital*, I.
12. *Ibid.*
13. Lucien Goldmann, "La Réification," *Les Temps modernes*, No. 156–57 (February–March, 1959).
14. *Ibid.*, p. 1449.
15. *Ibid.*, p. 1465.
16. Lucien Goldmann, "Propos dialectiques: Y a-t-il une sociologie marxiste?," *Les Temps modernes*, No. 140 (October, 1957), p. 743.
17. Karl Kautsky, "Introduction à l'ensemble du marxisme," in Karl Marx, *Le Capital* (Paris: Alfred Costes, 1949), I, xxiv.
18. Jean-Paul Sartre, "Questions de méthode," *Les Temps modernes* (September, 1957), p. 359.

19. Henri Lefebvre, *op. cit.*, pp. 128–37, and *Problèmes actuels du marxisme* (Paris: Presses Universitaires de France, 1958), pp. 45–52.

20. Marx, "Preface to the second edition," *Capital*, I, pp. 24–25.

21. V. I. Lenin, *Materialism and Empirio-Criticism* (New York: International Publishers, 1927), p. 220.

22. Marx and Engels, "Second Thesis on Feuerbach," in appendix to *The German Ideology* (New York: International Publishers, 1939), p. 197.

23. Marx, "Preface to the second edition," *Capital*, I, p. 25.

24. Karl Marx, *The Poverty of Philosophy* (New York: International Publishers, undated), p. 89.

25. Friedrich Engels, *Anti-Dühring* (Chicago: Charles H. Kerr & Co., 1907), p. 121.

26. Marx, "Preface to the second edition," *Capital*, I, p. 25.

27. See J. B. S. Haldane, *The Marxist Philosophy and the Sciences* (New York: Random House, 1939).

28. Karl Marx, "Critique of Hegel's Dialectic," in *Karl Marx: Early Writings*, 3rd manuscript, p. 206.

29. See Claude Cuenot, *Pierre Teilhard de Chardin* (Paris: Club des Editeurs, 1962), p. 467.

30. Quoted by Cuenot in *Le dernier symposium de la Wenner-Gren Foundation*, June, 1962.

31. Letter of September 21, 1952.

32. Pierre Teilhard de Chardin, *Le Phenomène humain*. The English translation by Bernard Wall is entitled *The Phenomenon of Man* (London: Collins; New York: Harper & Bros., 1959).

33. Teilhard de Chardin, *Les Singularités de l'espèce humaine* (Paris: Masson), pp. 48–49.

34. Michel Bosquet, *L'Express*, June 4, 1959, p. 24.

35. See Henri Lefebvre, *La Somme et le reste* (Paris: La Nef de Paris); Pierre Fougeyrollas, *Le Marxisme en question* (Paris: Editions du Seuil); and Edgar Morin, *Autocritique* (Paris: Julliard).

36. Quoted by Vène, *op. cit.*, p. 345.

37. Nilakanta Sastri, "L'Avenir des cultures traditionnelles," *Chronique de l'UNESCO*, May, 1959.

38. Placide Tempels, *La Philosophie bantoue* (Paris: Présence Africaine, 1949); Marcel Griaule, *Dieu d'eau* (Paris: Editions du Chene, 1948); and Roland Colin, *Les Contes de l'Ouest Africain* (Paris: Présence Africaine, 1957).

39. L. J. Lebret, *Suicide ou survie de l'Occident* (Paris: Editions ouvrières, 1958), pp. 37–140.

40. Georges Balandier, *Le Tiers Monde* (Paris: Presses Universitaires de France, 1956).

41. Kautsky, *op. cit.*, p. lxi.

42. François Perroux, "Une Nation en voie de se faire: la République de Guinée," *Revue de l'Action populaire*, No. 120 (June, 1959), pp. 683–705.

43. *Ibid.*, p. 704.

The African Road to Socialism

1. Jean-Paul Sartre, "Preface," in Senghor (ed.), *Anthologie de la nouvelle poésie nègre et malgache de langue française* (Paris: Presses Universitaires de France, 1948).

2. Vincent Monteil, *Les Musulmans soviétiques* (Paris: Editions du Seuil, 1957).

3. Engels, *Anti-Dühring*, p. 21.

4. Gaëtan Picon, *Panorama des idées contemporaines* (Paris: Gallimard, 1957). See also Gaston Bachelard, *Le nouvel esprit scientifique* (Paris: Presses Universitaires de France, 1946), and Pierre Guaydier, *Les grandes découvertes de la physique moderne* (Paris: Corrêa, 1951).

5. Picon, *op. cit.*, p. 11.

6. *Ibid.*, pp. 25, 26.

7. *Ibid.*, p. 27.

8. See Haldane, *The Marxist Philosophy and the Sciences*.

9. Engels, *Anti-Dühring*, p. 19.

10. *Ibid.*, pp. 18–22.

11. Maurice Leenhardt, "Ethnologie de la parole," *Cahiers internationaux de sociologie*, I (1946).

12. Geneviève Calame-Griaule and Blaise Calame, "Introduction à l'étude de la musique africaine," *La Revue musicale*, p. 238.

13. For the importance of word and symbol in Black Africa, see Marcel Griaule, *Dieu d'eau*, pp. 15, 25, 27–28, 34, 46, 60, 73, 80. See also Leo Frobenius, *Histoire de la Civilisation africaine* (Paris: Gallimard, 1936), and Tempels, *La Philosophie bantoue*.

14. See my lecture entitled "La Préhistoire et les groupes ethniques."

15. Though I do not share all his views—he underestimates Negro-African civilization—this is what Georges Gusdorf has done in "Colonisation et décolonisation," *Le Monde non-chrétien*, pp. 49–50.

16. V. I. Lenin, *Selected Works in Two Volumes* (Moscow: Foreign Languages Publishing House, 1950), I, Part 2, pp. 317–86.

17. *Ibid.*, p. 370.

18. Maurice Delafosse, *Les Civilisations négro-africaines* (Paris: Stock, 1925).

The Theory and Practice of Senegalese Socialism

1. Engels, *Dialectics of Nature* (New York: International Publishers, 1940).

2. Bachelard, *op. cit.*, p. 12.

3. Paul Robert, *Dictionnaire alphabétique et analogique de la langue française* (Casablanca, Société du Nouveau Littré, 1953).

4. Henri Lefebvre, *Le Matérialisme dialectique* (Paris: Presses Universitaires de France, 1957), p. 142.

5. Marx, *The Poverty of Philosophy*, p. 90.

6. Bachelard, *Le nouvel esprit scientifique*, p. 40.

7. Engels, *Dialectics of Nature*, p. 27.

8. Marx, "Critique of Hegel's Dialectic," pp. 206, 208.

9. Engels, *Dialectics of Nature*, pp. 6, 9.

10. *Ibid.*, p. 17.

11. *Ibid.*, pp. 282–83.

12. *Ibid.*, p. 284.

13. *Ibid.*, p. 290.

14. *Ibid.*, p. 289.

15. Cited in Lefebvre, *Le Matérialisme dialectique*, pp. 143–44.

16. Marx, "Critique of Hegel's Dialectic," p. 208.

17. Marx, quoted by Lefebvre, *Le Matérialisme dialectique*, p. 136.

18. *Ibid.*, p. 138.
19. Marx, "Private Property and Communism," in *Karl Marx: Early Writings,* 3rd manuscript, p. 156.
20. Marx and Engels, *The German Ideology,* p. 41.
21. *Ibid.*, p. 40.
22. See Lefebvre, *Le Matérialisme dialectique,* p. 150.
23. Roger Garardy, *Les Fins de la morale marxiste* (Paris: Editions La Palabre), p. 173.
24. V. I. Lenin, speech of October 2, 1920, "The Tasks of the Youth Leagues" (Moscow-Leningrad Cooperative Publishing Society of Foreign Workers in the U.S.S.R., 1935), p. 14.
25. Marx, "Private Property and Communism," p. 167.
26. *Ibid.*, p. 163.
27. *Ibid.*, p. 155.
28. Gaston Berger, in *Revue Prospective,* No. 1, pp. 4, 6, 7.
29. *Ibid.*, No. 4, p. 7.
30. Marx, "Private Property and Communism," p. 162.
31. Quoted by Zakaria Ibrahim in "The Communism of the Future," *Orient,* No. 19.
32. Henri Lefebvre, *Le Marxisme* (Paris: Presses Universitaires de France, 1947), p. 99.
33. Engels, *Dialectics of Nature,* p. 19.
34. See Marx and Engels, *The German Ideology,* pp. 20–23.
35. Marx, "Private Property and Communism," p. 155.
36. See Marx, "Critique of Hegel's Dialectic," pp. 195–219.
37. Lefebvre, *Le Matérialisme dialectique,* p. 1.
38. Engels, *Dialectics of Nature,* pp. 206–7.
39. *Ibid.*, p. 26.
40. *Ibid.*, p. 216.
41. Lefebvre, *Le Matérialisme dialectique,* p. 9.
42. *Ibid.*, p. 10.
43. Engels, *Dialectics of Nature,* p. 207.
44. Lefebvre, *Le Matérialisme dialectique,* p. 14.
45. *Ibid.*, pp. 14–15.
46. Engels, *Dialectics of Nature,* p. 183.
47. Lefebvre, *Le Matérialisme dialectique,* p. 18.
48. Engels, *Dialectics of Nature,* p. 183.
49. Marx, "Critique of Hegel's Dialectic," p. 215.
50. Engels, *Dialectics of Nature,* p. 26.
51. Marx, "Preface to the second edition," *Capital,* I, 25.
52. Marx and Engels, "Eleven Theses on Feuerbach," in appendix to *The German Ideology,* pp. 197–99.
53. Engels, *Dialectics of Nature,* pp. 173–74.
54. Marx, "Preface to the second edition," *Capital,* I, 26.
55. See Lefebvre, *Le Marxisme,* pp. 29–30.
56. Engels, *Dialectics of Nature,* p. 19.
57. *Ibid.*, p. 296.
58. *Ibid.*, p. 293.
59. Ibrahim, "The Communism of the Future," p. 160.
60. Marx and Engels, *The German Ideology,* p. 15.

61. Lefebvre, *Le Marxisme,* p. 50.

62. Marx, "Private Property and Communism," p. 156.

63. Marx and Engels, *The German Ideology,* p. 41.

64. Lenin, "The Tasks of the Youth Leagues," p. 13.

65. Lefebvre, *Le Marxisme,* p. 57.

66. See Senghor, *Pierre Teilhard de Chardin et la politique africaine* (Paris: Editions du Seuil, 1962).

67. See Guaydier, *op. cit.*

68. Ahmed Fouad al Ahwani, "Nationalisme et Religion," *Orient,* No. 18, p. 186.

69. Marx, "Private Property and Communism," p. 167.

70. *Ibid.,* p. 164.

71. Teilhard de Chardin, *The Phenomenon of Man,* p. 29.

72. See Engels, *Dialectics of Nature,* pp. 1 ff.

73. Pierre Teilhard de Chardin, *Oeuvres,* II: *L'Apparition de l'homme* (Paris: Editions du Seuil, 1956).

74. Teilhard de Chardin, *Oeuvres: III: La Vision du passé* (Paris: Editions du Seuil, 1958), 307–8.

75. See Teilhard de Chardin, *The Phenomenon of Man,* pp. 40–52.

76. Teilhard de Chardin, *Oeuvres,* III, 312–13.

77. *Ibid.,* III, 94.

78. *Ibid.,* III, 41, 171–74.

79. *Ibid.,* II, 314.

80. *Ibid.,* II, 214.

81. *Ibid.,* II, 302.

82. *Ibid.,* III, 291.

83. *Ibid.,* II, 329.

84. Letter of September 27, 1952.

85. Teilhard de Chardin, *Oeuvres,* III, 294.

86. "Gaston Berger, le Philosophe de l'action," in *Hommage à Gaston Berger* (University of Dakar, 1962).

87. Teilhard de Chardin, *Oeuvres,* II, 333.

88. *Ibid.,* II, 338–39.

89. *Ibid.,* V: *L'Avenir de l'homme* (Paris: Editions du Seuil, 1959), 363.

90. Cited in Paul Chauchard, *Morale chrétienne et morale marxiste,* p. 69.

91. Engels, *Dialectics of Nature,* p. 7.

92. *Ibid.,* p. 25.

93. See Henri Lefebvre, *La Pensée de Lénine* (Paris: Bordas, 1957), pp. 304–8.

94. See my interview in the weekly *Gavroche,* August 8, 1946.

95. Gaston Berger, "Liberté, Indépendance, Développement," *Tiers-Monde,* No. 4, pp. 408–9.

96. *Ibid.,* p. 404.

97. Gaston Berger, in *Revue Prospective,* No. 5, p. 133.

98. Teilhard de Chardin, *Oeuvres,* V, VI.

99. *Ibid.,* V, 74.

100. *Ibid.,* VI, 181–86.

101. Marcel Griaule, *Dieu d'eau,* p. 29. This truth is confirmed by science. See Jean Rostand, *L'Hérédité humaine* (Paris: Presses Universitaires de France, 1952), pp. 53–54.

102. Calame-Griaule and Calame, "Introduction à l'étude de la musique africaine," p. 11.

103. See Maurice Merleau-Ponty, *Les Aventures de la dialectique* (Paris: Gallimard, 1955).

104. Lenin, *Materialism and Empirio-Criticism*, p. 128.

105. Engels, *Dialectics of Nature*, p. 172.

106. Lefebvre, *La Pensée de Lénine*, pp. 124, 128, 130.

107. Lenin, *Materialism and Empirio-Criticism*, p. 267.

108. Engels, *Dialectics of Nature*, p. 206.

109. Merleau-Ponty, *op. cit.*, p. 91.

110. Marx and Engels, "Eleven Theses on Feuerbach," p. 197.

111. Guaydier, *op. cit.*, p. 251.

112. Bachelard, *op. cit.*, p. 172.

113. See Teilhard de Chardin, *Oeuvres*, VI, 144.

114. Bachelard, *op. cit.*, p. 179.

115. *Ibid.*, p. 148.

116. Teilhard de Chardin, *The Phenomenon of Man*, pp. 40–63 *passim*.

117. *Ibid.*, p. 54.

118. *Loc. cit.*

119. *Ibid.*, pp. 57–60.

120. *Ibid.*, p. 61.

121. *Ibid.*, p. 64.

122. Teilhard de Chardin, *Oeuvres*, II, 363.

123. Merleau-Ponty, *op. cit.*, p. 89.

124. Senghor, "Socialisme africain et développement, ou la Voie sénégalaise," *Développement et Civilisation*, 1962.

125. Maurice Blondel, *Vocabulaire philosophique* (Paris: Presses Universitaires de France).

126. Gaston Berger, in *Revue Prospective*, No. 7, p. 111.

127. *Ibid.*, No. 1, pp. 3–4.

128. Lefebvre, *La Pensée de Lénine*, p. 118.

129. François Perroux, *L'Economie du XXᵉ siècle* (Paris: Presses Universitaires de France, 1961), p. 198.

130. *Ibid.*, p. 155.

131. Cited by Lefebvre, *La Pensée de Lénine*, p. 120.

132. *Ibid.*, p. 260.

133. Lenin, *Oeuvres choisies* (Moscow: Foreign Languages Publishing House), II, 197–98.

134. *Ibid.*, II, 1030.

135. Lefebvre, *Le Marxisme*, p. 53.

136. Marx, "Private Property and Labour," in *Karl Marx: Early Writings*, 3rd manuscript, p. 147.

137. Claude Tresmontant, *Morale chrétienne et morale marxiste*, pp. 190–93, *passim*.

138. Luke 4:18.

139. Koran 4:36.

140. Mustapha al Siba'f, "A propos du 'Socialisme de l'Islam,'" *Orient*, No. 20 (1961), p. 178.

141. Tresmontant, *op. cit.*, p. 207.

142. St. Basil, *Sermon on St. Luke,* cited in L. J. Lebret, *Suicide ou survie de l'Occident,* p. 361.

143. *Al Istiqlal,* June 11, 1960.

144. See Gilberto Freyre, *Maîtres et Esclaves* (Paris: Gallimard, 1952).

145. Werner Jaeger, *Early Christianity and the Greek Paideia* (Cambridge, Mass.: Belknap Press, 1961).

146. Edmond Ortigues, *Le Discours et le symbole* (Paris: Editions Montaigne), p. 9.